WHO MOVED?

When you feel distant from God, who moved?

The contents of this work including, but not limited to, the accuracy of events, people, and places depicted; opinions expressed; permission to use previously published materials included; and any advice given or actions advocated are solely the responsibility of the author, who assumes all liability for said work and indemnifies the publisher against any claims stemming from publication of the work.

All Rights Reserved
Copyright © 2019 by Denis Dion

No part of this book may be reproduced or transmitted, downloaded, distributed, reverse engineered, or stored in or introduced into any information storage and retrieval system, in any form or by any means, including photocopying and recording, whether electronic or mechanical, now known or hereinafter invented without permission in writing from the publisher.

RoseDog Books
585 Alpha Drive, Suite 103
Pittsburgh, PA 15238
Visit our website at www.rosedogbookstore.com

ISBN: 978-1-6453-0562-0
eISBN: 978-1-6453-0368-8

WHO MOVED?

By
Denis Dion

With contributions by
Anna May Dion

PITTSBURGH, PENNSYLVANIA 15238

Table of Contents

Foreword by Christopher Dion vii
Introduction ix

Chapter 1: The Magi 1
Chapter 2: The Prodigal Son 11
Chapter 3: What God Wants 17
Chapter 4: Come and See 23
Chapter 5: My Shepherd 29
Chapter 6: Lost Sheep 35
Chapter 7: Doubt & Unbelief 39
Chapter 8: Open Door 51
Chapter 9: Wealth & Comfort 61
Chapter 10: Rock Bottom 69
Chapter 11: David & Peter 85
Chapter 12: Marriage: Walking Together 93
Chapter 13: What God Wants 101
Chapter 14: Obey, Trust, Love 107
Chapter 15: In the Palm of His Hand 113
Chapter 16: Another Journey 121
Chapter 17: God-Still You 127
Chapter 18: Another Mother-in-law 131
Chapter 19: Calling Us Back 135
Chapter 20: The Be-attitudes 139

Epilogue 151

Foreword

"Dawn"

By
Christopher Dion

I'm here. I don't know why I'm here. I never did like this park. It is only two blocks from my house, and yet I have only been here three times before. You see, McNulty Park is like an oil painting done by a ten-year-old. From far away, it looks good. There are healthy, green trees; short, stout, full pine bushes; soft looking, green thick grass; stout benches; all surrounded by a short, strong cement walk. However, up close, the painting, and the park, lose their beauty. From nowhere, beer bottles spring up like weeds; broken glass clings to the walkway like splattered bugs; sections of boards, torn from the park benches, lay strewn amongst the bushes like fallen victims of some lost battle; newspapers blow around the park like so many scattered leaves; and words are scrawled on the cement wall in assorted colors of paint like a mangled, disfigured rainbow. Looking eastward over the wall, I see the Connecticut River with so many factories looming into the darkness, spewing their waste into the air and water. Behind me, the traffic begins to pick up on the busy street that runs by the park. A few trucks rumble by, their engines making deafening noises. No, up close this place is certainly not pretty. In fact, it is a complete mess. What am I doing here? No answer comes except for the brightening of the sky.

I came here on impulse. I got home from work at 5:00 am and decided to come down. I reasoned that I should be more familiar with the park that is so close to my house. Maybe it had changed. Maybe someone had cleaned it up. Not maybe. I was wrong. Definitely, I was wrong. But why do I continue to stand here? The wind is biting, and my thin jacket is not keeping me very warm. The bugs are everywhere, and they are driving me insane. The smell from the trash all over the ground and the different pollutants around is really awful. What am I doing here?

In reply, the quiet, cottony clouds turn vivid orange and red.

Well, who knows? I heard someone say once that nothing ever just happens. Maybe there is a reason for me to be in this awful place. Maybe God wants me to be here. God. I haven't thought about Him much lately, never mind talk to Him. For some reason, I've just been letting Him slip away. I know He is still out there somewhere, but I just haven't been taking the time to be with Him. Maybe God has something to say to me today. Is that why I'm here?

To answer, the sun sneaks over the horizon, brightening the day.

Wow! Just look at all this beauty! The sun lights up the dew on the leaves of the trees and the deep green grass. The light glitters off the glass on the walkways like so many diamonds on the ground. The sun lights up the water of the river forming little sparkles on the water like a million tiny aqua stars. The brightness manifests the pure, white clouds and clean, clear blue sky. Just look at all this! Who can live with such beauty and say there is no God? Of course there is a God. And He must love me a lot to give me all these wonderful things! OK God. I get the message. I've strayed far enough. I'm going home. Home, to my house and to You.

Funny! This is the second time God has used a Son-rise to help me believe and love!

Introduction

In the past few years a popular expression has been, *"When you feel distant from God, who moved?"* It is intended to make the point that we are the ones who drift away from God; that God stays put. Just before the Christmas of 2013, I was lolling in bed on a Saturday morning and reflecting on how good God has been to me all my life; how He has been there for me every step of the way, and how, many times, I have not been there for Him. Who moved? Always me.

This book is not intended to be an autobiography, but much of my life is shared from chapter to chapter. Knowing that I am not unique and not the only sinner on planet Earth, I'm hoping that by sharing with you the many ways I have moved away from God's providential care, then back again, it will help you understand why, at times, you may feel very distant from God, while at other times you feel so close to Him that your heart seems to be bursting with joy. Doesn't that make you want to stay within whispering distance of the Shepherd?

CHAPTER 1
THE MAGI

Matthew 2: 1-12

After Jesus' birth in Bethlehem in Judea during the reign of King Herod, astrologers from the East arrived one day in Jerusalem inquiring, "Where is the new born king of the Jews? We observed his star at its rising and have come to pay him homage." At this news King Herod became very disturbed, and with him all Jerusalem. Summoning all of the chief priests and scribes of the people, he inquired of them where the Messiah was to be born. "In Bethlehem of Judea," they informed him. "Here is what the prophet has written:

'And you, Bethlehem of Judah, are by no means least among the princes of Judah, since from you shall come a ruler who is to shepherd my people, Israel.'"

Herod called the astrologers aside and found out from them the exact time of the star's appearance. Then he sent them to Bethlehem, after instructing them: "Go and get detailed information about the child. When you have found him, report it to me so that I may go and offer him homage too."

In reading Holy Scripture, from Genesis to the Book of Revelation, it becomes obvious that in our relationship with God, He is the stable one. God is everywhere all the time. Thus, He doesn't move. There isn't anywhere for Him to go since He's already there. So when I feel distant from God, it has to be me who moved, who decided to turn away from Him, spiritually and emotionally. It is my decision, not His, to put distance between us. Over the past few years I've been thinking a lot about this yo-yo movement between God and me and find some of the reasons very interesting, with inspiring stories and events. The decisions that put distance between God and me are often sinful; sins that I commit or sins of omission; things that I should have done but didn't do; negative attitudes, disinterest, and indifference. I usually become aware of my moving either away from or toward God through Holy Scripture, retreats, spiritual workshops, or good sermons.

Over the past few years, the best way for me to see where I stand with God is in the reflections I write after reading Holy Scripture (Lectio Divina). When I'm honest with myself and when I allow the Holy Spirit to guide my thoughts, these reflections give me a really good sense of who I am and in which direction I am moving. I've come to realize how important it is to recognize the joy and peace that come from being one with God, as well as the sadness, the internal turmoil, and unrest of being out of touch with Him. It is an ongoing back-and-forth process, and I am constantly praying for ways to remain close to Him, to live in the *"God Zone."* I was made aware of this term at a workshop on the Beatitudes given by two professors from a local Catholic college. The *"God Zone"* is living in total peace, joy and freedom from all distractions, turmoil, friction, injustice, and all the bad stuff of the world that keeps me from being close to God. When I'm in the *"God Zone,"* I don't want to move out. But life happens, and once again I start to inch out little by little. Sometimes I snap right back, sometimes not. I'm sure you are familiar with that pattern, so let's get down to business and see what we can find in the Bible to help us with these yo-yo-like comings and goings. Notice I switched from the first-person singular to the first-person plural. I include myself in all of this, but I want you to feel part of this book also.

Let us begin with one of the great stories of moving toward God, specifically, Jesus. We find this story in Matthew 2: 1-12. It is the story of a group of astrologers who notice a new star in the heavens. They turn to their books, and, O Heavens! This star tells them a very special King will be born unto the world, somewhere West of where they live. I can see them now sharing with each other their best guesses as to which kingdom will be honored by the birth of a child so special that a new star should herald his coming. Nowhere in their books did it tell them that the star would shine above the location of the birth. Undaunted, they gathered their resources and assembled a caravan. If faith could be measured, I can't imagine the amount it would take to plan a voyage not knowing where you are going, how far you are going and how long you will be gone. All you know is that a star in the sky will guide you.

My wife Anna May and I are not very good travelers. I love flying; she doesn't. We did manage to travel to a few places during the fifty-plus years we've been married, but as much as we love being in places we've never seen before, getting there is not usually a pleasant experience for us. That is why I find the journey undertaken by the Magi such a gargantuan effort, willingly entered into by these unique individuals. The finances and the logistics of it alone, I find overwhelming. It boggles my mind when I think about everything that was needed to organize a caravan of that size. In July of 2014, we attended a family reunion in Colorado. We live in Massachusetts. We were only going to be away for nine days, and we began planning the trip in November of 2013. As I said, we don't travel much, and we wanted to make sure every "t" was crossed and every "i" dotted. It is very obvious to me that the Magi spared no expense, no amount of energy to make the journey that would bring them to Jesus. What a great lesson that is for me. I have to ask, "How hard do I work at coming to Jesus? How much effort do I make in assessing exactly where I stand with God? Have I distanced myself from Him? If so, what do I plan to do about it? Do I even want to do something about it, and if so, what must I do to begin my move closer to Him? How do I put together the *caravan* of courage it takes sometimes to move back into His presence? The Magi were planning a journey that would take months, maybe even years, to come to Christ. For me, it can happen in the amount of time it takes to say, "*I'm sorry, Lord. Please forgive me.*"

These astrologers, known to us as the Magi, would come to Jesus. They were not Jewish, so there's a good chance they were not familiar with the prophecies and promises of the God of Israel and His vow to send His people a Messiah, a Savior, and how this Messiah would come into the world. Despite all that, they were determined to seek Him. They set out heading West, having no idea who and what they would encounter along the way. I'm certain they took their precautions and traveled with a select troop of warriors to protect them, for they were laden with many provisions as well as the gifts for this Child once they found Him. They had no idea how long the journey would take and what types of climates they would encounter. They moved ahead, ever closer to the Divine. Was that the reason they marched on so steadfastly? They couldn't have known the Child they sought was God, yet they never faltered. I know Jesus is God, so I am not surprised by the joy I feel when I am in His presence and how good I feel about doing the Father's will. There's a special excitement within me when I hear the whispers of the Holy Spirit and how good I feel when I allow myself to be used by God, even if I can't see down the road what it is He wants me to accomplish.

Did the Magi travel by night? Was the star so bright it was visible even in daylight? We don't know. We do know they continued to move closer and closer to the Son of God. Twenty, thirty, maybe forty miles a day, they came to pay homage to a foreign king. A caravan of that size would have traveled slower than a smaller group. Time mattered not. They moved on. Was God the Father watching over them, keeping them on course, keeping them safe, even from the evil Herod? After all, these Magi were part of His plan. They must have encountered setbacks such as bad weather, stormy skies when they would lose sight of the star; frustrating barriers, such as mountains and chasms and rivers which seemingly could not be crossed. There must have been deserts, and deep woods, uncharted mountains and plains, no roads, or paths, or passages to follow, and definitely no GPS. Does that sound like the ingredients of your life? Yet, the Magi never turned back. They continued on their journey to the stable. I wonder if they had known that this King they were seeking would be found lying in an animal manger in a stable; if so, would they have sought Him out anyway? The star could not tell them that. The star told them only one thing—which way to set their compass. They kept going, seeking Emmanuel, God with us.

I have a compass, too, a moral compass. Very often, I ignore that compass and head out in a different direction, away from God. Did the Magi ever doubt or ignore their compass, the Star? Not as long they could see it. But, at one point they did lose sight of it, and they found a palace! That was encouraging, so, they stopped and inquired about the new king. Little did they know, they were talking to the one who was already the king of this area, but not exactly a good guy to be talking to. That pretty much happens to me, too. When I stray from The Way, I can end up talking to people I shouldn't be listening to, people who can lead me further away from the path I should be on. Fortunately, through His grace, I see God's hand extended out to me, beckoning me to return, to repent, to come to the stable, humbly where God, in all humility, lies waiting for me ready to embrace me and wrap me in His love.

Again, God was truly watching over these travelers, just as He watches over us when we seek to be in His presence. Herod didn't stop them. He even helped them and told them that Bethlehem was where they needed to go, then, instructed them to return and let him know exactly where this baby-king could be found. They resumed their journey, continuing to get ever closer to the Wonder Counselor! They had to know they were getting closer and that soon their journey would end, for once again, the star came out more vivid and brighter than before. Matthew describes their excitement.

"The star which they had observed at its rising went ahead of them until it came to a standstill over the place where the child was. They were overjoyed at seeing the star and on entering the house, found the child with Mary, his mother."
(Matthew 2: 9-10)

How did they know this was the king they were looking for? They were in a stable for heaven's sakes! They knew! Just as we all know when we are in the presence of God. The feeling is unmistakable. We all know what it's like to leave from a dark place and travel through pain and suffering and near spiritual death, plodding along not knowing if we are heading in the right direction, and finally coming into the Light and finding God there with arms wide open, waiting to embrace us and welcome us back. He hadn't moved. However, He is moved to tears to have us move back into His arms once again.

I think this is the perfect place for my wife Anna May to share with you a very inspiring journey:

There was a period during the late 1970s when my faith was challenged. Life was busy, and I became very disillusioned—

with marriage, family, life in general, and God. My inner self was churning with every negative emotion one can imagine. I was at war within myself and with Denis, and yes, even with God, to the point where I was beginning to doubt God's existence. Despite my doubts, there was a voice deep within me that kept saying, "Find me." I looked for him as I volunteered in a children's summer Bible class, attended weekly Mass, as well as in our own home Bible study, but He eluded me. I became increasingly discouraged, and that discouragement eventually led to a very serious disagreement with Denis.

During the disagreement, my head kept telling my mouth to be silent, but my mouth just kept shouting at him. I didn't want to say the things that I was saying, but a power within me wouldn't let me stop! Denis went straight to our room and wrote his feelings to me in his journal, which I read later. Reading it just made me angrier, and that really scared me because Denis was my rock, and if I had managed to bring him down into my darkness, how would we survive?

The next day, I sat with pen in hand and began to write my feelings to share with him. As I wrote, the words "Satan has been working overtime in our relationship," appeared on the page. At that moment, my eyes were opened, and I recognized that all of my inner churnings were the work of Satan and that he had brought me to the verge of committing the "sin against the Spirit."

I began to sob uncontrollably, and as I did so, I felt God wrap me in his arms. He held me tightly but gently as my tears washed away all of the inner turmoil and allowed God to replace it with an incredible sense of peace! Over the space of a couple of years, I had moved away from God, yet in an instant, He brought me back home. I knew at that moment that I had experienced a major conversion and that I would never be the same again. I now recognize the voice calling me to "find Him" as my baptismal grace at work. Satan worked hard at challenging me, but God's grace saved me. Praise God!

How did it happen that the distance between Anna May and God had gotten so great? I don't know. I don't think Anna May knows either. Both of us were very busy with our children and other family members at that time, and so it is possible God was almost an afterthought. And that is all Satan needs. He can crawl into the tiniest of cracks in our relationship with God and manages to pry us away if we are not paying attention. However, as Anna May's experience proves, we must always continue to seek Him, to want Him, to be attentive to His divine influence. Here is part of a meditation entitled *"Attentive to the Divine Influence."* This meditation appeared in the *Magnificat* magazine on December 13, 2013 and was written by Father John Tauler, o.p.(1361) a German Dominican priest, a popular 14th century preacher and mystical theologian. He wrote:

> *Be sure of this, children; there is not a single instant in which God does not pour into us some divine influence, which we would plainly feel if we were more attentive; for God is borne on by his nature to communicate himself unceasingly, and the nature of our spirit is formed to receive him.*

It is when turning a deaf ear to God, we convince ourselves that God cannot and does not want to forgive us and bring us back to Him that we fall to the unforgivable sin against the Spirit. With God, nothing is impossible, and that has to be the anchor of truth that stops us from drifting away into oblivion.

During that time in Anna May's life, I prayed very hard for her. Down deep, I knew she would *move* back and return to God. Like the father of the *"Prodigal Son,"* I kept watch, praying, hoping, believing.

CHAPTER 2

THE PRODIGAL SON

<u>Luke 15: 11-24</u>

Jesus said to them: "A man had two sons. The younger of them said to the father, 'Give me the share of the estate that is coming to me.' So the father divided the property. Some days later the younger son collected all his belongings and went off to a distant land, where he squandered his money on dissolute living. After he had spent everything, a great famine broke out in that country and he was in dire need. So he attached himself to one of the propertied class of the place, who sent him to his farm to take care of the pigs. He longed to fill his belly with the husks that were fodder for the pigs, but no one made a move to give him anything. Coming to his senses at last, he said: 'How many hired hands at my father's place have more than enough to eat, while here I am starving! I will break away and return to my father, and say to him, Father, I have sinned against God and against you; I no longer deserve to be called your son. Treat me like one of your hired hands.' With that he set off for his father's house. While he was still a long way off, his father caught sight of him and was deeply moved. He ran out to meet him, threw his arms around his neck, and kissed him. The son said to him: 'Father I have sinned against God and against you; I no longer deserve to be called your son.' The father said to his servants; 'Quick! Bring out the finest robe and put it on him; put a ring on his finger and shoes on his feet. Take the fatted calf and kill it. Let us eat and celebrate because this son of mine was dead and has come back to life. He was lost and is found.'"

Jesus was dining with tax collectors, sinners, Pharisees, and scribes, quite a group, and was trying to get them to understand God the Father's great mercy. He started telling stories that would make that point. The story of the Prodigal Son hits home with most families. It's a classic and fits in beautifully with the theme of this book, how we move away from God and come back again. It is also a very familiar reality with most families. It's nothing new. Even if we have not had the personal experience of either, being the prodigal son or daughter or being the parent of one or the other ourselves, we know someone who has. In fact, Jesus himself, at the age of twelve, chose to separate himself from his earthly father and mother and stayed in Jerusalem while they headed back home to Nazareth. It wasn't until a few days later Mary and Joseph realized he wasn't around and returned to the city to find him. Of course, that's a bit different because of who he was, but the experience was the same as any another parent for Mary and Joseph.

Now back to the parable in the Gospel of Luke. We have a father who has two sons living and working the familial property. The youngest son decides to listen to the lure of the world far from the family home. The Father doesn't stop him. Instead, he gives the son his inheritance, knowing full well it won't last him very long, and watches him walk away whistling a wandering song. The father knows. It hurts, but he knows. He knows what the young man is in for. Turning your back on father, mother, or both, is never a good thing. Sooner or later, you come to realize the love they have for you. You may find someone else who loves you, but never as deeply and sincerely as Mom and Dad. As much as the father hurts watching his son walk down the road, he knows his son will, at some point in time, be in a world of pain himself. So, he keeps watch. Every day, he sits out on the front porch, rocking, waiting and watching.

In this parable, the father represents God, the Father. And the son, that's us, you and me. The son is happy. He's got a pocket full of money and a head full of expectations. Life was going to be fun for a change. His heart is happy and light, and he feels he's doing the right thing. Taking care of the animals and digging in dirt was not his thing. He's got the world on a string, and he intends to make it his lifelong toy. As he moves further and further away from the father, he finds more people like himself who offer him the life he was looking for: wine, women, and song. Isn't life just great! He moves even further away from the father, and life keeps getting better and better. Then one day he reaches into his pocket to buy a drink, and his pocket is empty. Oops. Now what? Couldn't call home back then. No smart phones, not even dumb ones. No e-mails, no texts, no tweets, and no ATMs. He had moved very far away at this point. It wasn't until he was very hungry and thirsty that he decided to get a job. What could he do? Take care of animals and dig the dirt for growing stuff. He had moved very far away from that. And he was about to move even further away. He never had to look for a job before, so I'm sure he bumbled through a few interviews at first, then got so desperate he had to humiliate himself and beg for a job.

"I can take care of your pigs," he said. The pay wasn't much, and the food was the same as the pigs.

One day sitting in the muck of the sty, he heard this voice, his father's voice.

"I'm still watching for you. I love you, and I know you love me."

At first, he didn't pay too much attention. Had he been working out in the sun too long? But day after day of working harder and harder and eating less and less as the food got worse and worse, he began to pay attention to the little voice deep within his heart.

Coming to his senses at last, he said, "How many hired hands at my father's place have more than enough to eat, while here I am starving. I will break away and return to my father."
(Luke 15:17-18)

The young man, responding to the voice he heard, began the long trek back home. It seemed like he had been gone forever. He had doubts. He was afraid. He knew his father could get angry. He had been the brunt of his anger a few times, especially when he goofed off and then blamed his older brother for the work not getting done or the tool that was broken. But even though he was totally humiliated and even though his father might not want him back, the voice in his heart gave him the courage to at least beg for his father's forgiveness. He was moving back. Forgiveness. Oh gosh, how he longed to be forgiven. He wanted that more than anything. Even if he had to work as the lowest servant on his father's farm, didn't matter. What he sought now, longed for, hoped for, was forgiveness. If he only knew the Father always forgives. This father anyway. The Father Jesus was talking about. The father saw the son way before the son saw the father, way before the son realized that he was close enough to home to be seen. By the time he got there, the welcoming party was already being organized. Forgiven? Yes, by all means. The warm embrace, the flowing tears, the sound of his name on his father's lips were more than he could have imagined, after what he had done.

Jesus was telling all these sinners and doubters what His Father was like. He was telling them, no matter how lost you might think you are, the Father is out there on the front porch waiting for you to move back in. Jesus told that story so that today, you and I would want to know His Father better, know Him well enough to never want to move away from Him.

It's not every son that gets hugged by his father. My dad was not into hugging men, even his sons. I was in my teens before my father hugged me. My older brother and I were away at school. It was a high school level seminary in New Hampshire. Our home was more than three hours away in Massachusetts. Visiting days were limited to one Sunday every other month. The only holiday we were able to get home for was Christmas and New Year's. From September to Christmas wasn't too bad, but from January to June was a bit tougher, for us as well as for my folks. On one of my parent's visits in the spring, as soon as my dad was out of the car, he grabbed me and gave me the biggest hug. I'll never forget it. Being away is tough, even moving away for a legitimate reason. After four years, I left that school and moved back home. I told my parents I wanted to join the Air Force.

My dad shook his head and said, *"OK. But not right now. You've been away for four years. Stick around for a while?"*

You see, when we move away, we're not the only ones who feel bad. The Father does too. A year later, it happened again. This time, I went away to school in Boston. That was only 100 miles away, and I was able to take the bus back home every weekend. Less than a year later, I got a job in Vermont, and once again, I had moved further away. Coming home on my days off was great. I did that for close to a year. When I was home, it was wonderful. But even though I enjoyed my work, being away was difficult. Today, I see this back and forth experience as exactly what happens in my spiritual life. I love being close to God. There is no greater feeling than the joy of being in His presence. It is a joy that is beyond happiness.

In fact, joy and happiness are two very different things. Happiness is from the world, while joy is happiness in God. As I distance myself from God, I cease to feel joyful. I can still be happy to a certain extent. For example, when I'm at a sporting event, and my team is winning, I'm happy, even very happy. When my children and grandchildren come to visit, that makes me very happy, no matter how close or how distant I am from God. Joy, on the other hand is when I feel loved and accepted by God and when I know I have His forgiveness. I can feel His Spirit within me, and there is no other feeling like it in the world. The love I have for Anna May and knowing she loves me comes close, but that is happiness, not joy. My goal then, should be to stay as close to God as possible, for as long as possible.

It isn't easy. There are so many factors that come into play during the course of a day. The main enemy, of course, is Satan. He throws so much junk at us intending to push us away from God. If he can manage it, he loves pushing downhill. What helps me a lot lately in the battle against the devil is not wanting to live without that feeling of joy I experience when I am close to God. I don't want to put distance between us. When I do, I feel like that prodigal son, wallowing in the pigsty, just wanting so badly to get back home. Unlike the prodigal son, I know the Father is on the front porch watching for me.

CHAPTER 3

WHAT GOD WANTS

1Samuel 8: 4-18

All the elders of Israel came in a body to Samuel at Ramah and said to him. "Now that you are old, and your sons do not follow your example, appoint a king over us, as other nations have, to judge us."

Samuel was displeased when they asked for a king to judge them. He prayed to the Lord, however, who said in answer: "Grant the people's every request. It is not you they reject, they are rejecting me as their king. As they have treated me constantly from the day I brought them up from Egypt to this day, deserting me and worshipping strange gods, so do they treat you too. Now, grant their request: but at the same time, warn them solemnly and inform them of the rights of the king who will rule them."

Samuel delivered the message of the Lord in full to those who were asking him for a king. He told them: "The rights of the king are as follows: He will take your sons and assign them to his chariots and horses, and they will run before his chariot. He will also appoint from among them his command-

> *ers of groups of a thousand and of a hundred soldiers. He will set them to do his plowing and his harvesting and to make his implements of war and the equipment of his chariots. He will use his daughters as ointment-makers, as cooks, and as bakers. He will take the best of your fields, vineyards, and olive groves, and give them to his officials. He will tithe your crops and your vineyards and give the revenue to his eunuchs and his slaves. He will take your male and female servants, as well as your best oxen and your asses, and use them to do his work. He will tithe your flocks and you yourselves will become his slaves. When this takes place, you will complain against the king whom you have chosen, but on that day the Lord will not answer you.*

From the very beginning, people have moved away from God, then embraced Him, then moved away again, and again, and again. It happened to Adam and Eve, and their children, and their children's children. It still occurs today. I do that, and I believe anyone reading this will admit they do that, too. It's the process of sinning against God and neighbor, feeling bad about what we've done or didn't do, or even thought and desired, repenting and turning back, then asking for and receiving forgiveness. This is nothing new. It dates back to even before the *Garden* and Adam and Eve. It goes back to Lucifer and his band of angels who rebelled against God and were thus expelled from Heaven and the Divine presence. However, the difference between the devils and us is that we have been Redeemed by the Death and Resurrection of Jesus and through divine grace are given the courage, the strength, the inspiration, the sincerity of heart and desire to come back before God and ask for forgiveness. And we stand forgiven. So, it is an old story that continues today and will go on until the end of time.

Holy Scripture is filled with glaring examples of both people moving away and coming back. We all are familiar with what went on in the desert after Moses, with God's help, led the people of God out of bondage in Egypt and intended to bring them to a Promised Land, a land flowing with *milk and honey*. To get there, they had to cross the desert. Things were pretty good for a while. Eventually the people began grumbling and complaining, moving away from God, when the food supplies started to run short. Moses talked to God about it, and God sent them food and water, every day. The people were satisfied. They moved back. Then God called Moses and wanted to talk at the top of Mt. Sinai. That's when God gave him the Ten Commandments, but it took a while, forty days in fact. When Moses came back down, he found his people had moved very far away from God and were worshiping a golden calf. Again, Moses reconciled the group, but as punishment, God kept them in that desert for 40 years. During that time, God's people continued to vacillate back and forth, a process that continues to this day. We can't point our finger and click our tongue in accusation of the Israelites, for we do the same thing. One minute we embrace God with all our heart, mind, and soul, and the next minute we're in love with a "golden calf," the world and all its pitfalls. Our attention span with God is very short.

The Exodus from Egypt is not the only example we have of God's people abandoning Him and His precepts. Let us fast forward a few centuries and catch up with the prophet Samuel. In the first book of Samuel, chapter 8, God and the prophet are having a conversation. Samuel is telling God the people want Him to anoint a king. Up until that time, Judges, appointed by God through various holy people such as prophets and the Levites, the priestly people, had governed the Israelites. For some reason now the people were not satisfied with that. They looked around them and found other nations led by kings who grew very powerful and threatened their tiny Nation. Fear, one of the great enemies of faith, brought them to Samuel demanding that, they, too, needed a king in order to defend themselves. They did not believe anymore that God could and would protect them. They were moving away from God, far away. No matter what Samuel said, they insisted. Here's what the elders of Israel told him,

> *"Now that you are old and your sons do not follow your example, appoint a king over us as other nations have to judge us."* (1 Samuel 8: 4-5)

Samuel was none too happy because he knew he'd have to talk to God about this, who, he knew, was none too happy about this either. But Samuel, true to his calling, prayed. And true to His promise, God answered. Sam was right. God was very angry, and the conversation between the two was not very pretty. (1 Samuel 8:6-22) God was looking at an entire nation moving away from Him. That had to hurt. God doesn't force us to stay close to Him. He has given us free will and never, ever takes it back. So, He didn't argue with Samuel, but He did give him a message to take back to the people with the hope that it would change their minds.

He told Samuel, *"Grant the people's every request. It is not you they reject, it is me they are rejecting as their king."* God didn't stop there. Basically what He said to Samuel was, *"Go ahead. Appoint a king. They'll be sorry, because you know what. I know human nature better than all of you. The king will be good for a while until he realizes how much power he has. And you know what, absolute power corrupts absolutely. Oh, will they ever be sorry then. The king will not only tax them, he'll grab their sons, their husbands, their land, their farms, their vineyards, their homes; they will become slaves; they will experience terrible wars. Rest assured Sam, they will complain, and you go back and tell the people this;*

"When this takes place, you will complain against the king whom you have chosen, but on that day the Lord will not answer you." (1 Samuel 8:18)

What we have to know about this passage is, though it occurred centuries and centuries ago, God doesn't feel any differently about us than He did about His chosen people. God is not an evolving deity. God is God, then, now, and forever. He is Almighty, All Everything. There is no room for improvement. He already is everything there is to be to the most complete degree. So, when we insist we are right because the times are very different from when Jesus walked the earth, think again. You want to walk away, turn away from His love and care? Go right ahead. But don't complain when the wings fall off and your plane crashes.

Now, you might say to me, *"God is all merciful, all loving, all forgiving, and all I have to do is feel sincerely sorry for my transgression and beg His forgiveness, and through His mercy I will be forgiven."*

OK. If that is how you truly feel, that is the sin of *"presumption."* You are presuming that you can go and lead a life of sin and that at the moment of your death you will have a miraculous change of heart, repent, and with your dying breath be saved. I've got news for you. That's not how God works. Let me say this. If one believes that about God, forgiving a lifetime of sin and faithless living at the very last moment, then one must believe in God. And if one believes in God, then one must believe there is a hell. And if there is a hell, who is it for if all are given one last moment to beg His forgiveness? Just sayin'. Besides, one doesn't know how or when death will come. One could get hit from behind by a bus and not have a single moment to repent. We have free will. We are given the freedom to choose a life of grace or a life of sin. Yes, it is true that if we choose a life of grace we will sin anyway, but a grace filled conscience will never rest peacefully until given pardon for the transgression. In Hebrew, the word "repent" means "to turn." When we sin, we move away from God. When we repent, we turn back toward God and move nearer to Him. It is really to our advantage to use our free will wisely, and try our best to make the proper choices, choices that will please God and keep us within His loving embrace.

CHAPTER 4

COME AND SEE

John 1: 35-42

The next day John was there again with two of his disciples. As he watched Jesus walk by he said, "Look! There is the Lamb of God!" The two disciples heard what he said, and followed Jesus. When Jesus turned around and noticed them following him, he asked them, "What are you looking for?" They said to him, "Rabbi (which means Teacher) where do you stay?" "Come and see," he answered. So they went to see where he was lodged, and stayed with him that day. One of the two who had followed him after hearing John was Simon Peter's brother Andrew. The first thing he did was seek out his brother Simon and tell him, "We have found the Messiah!" (This term means the Anointed). He brought him to Jesus, who looked at him and said, "You are Simon son of John; your name shall be Cephas (which is rendered Peter)."

One of my favorite sayings, a warning actually, is *"Don't play chess with God. You will lose every time."* John 1: 35-42 is a typical passage from John the Evangelist, only seven verses, and God is playing chess. The pieces involve His Son, Jesus, John the Baptist, and some of his followers. In this passage from John's Gospel, God the Father sees to it that His Son and "The Baptist" come within shouting distance of each other. As they cross paths, John, true to the prophets, proclaims, *"Behold, the Lamb of God."* He was with two of his disciples, one of whom was Andrew, who leaves John and goes and gets his brother, Peter, and they proceed to meet Jesus. They leave John right then and there to follow "The One," the classic move toward Jesus. This happens throughout my life. I hear a good sermon, or attend a workshop, or go on a retreat and most times I can actually feel my heart opening up and moving closer and closer to the Divine presence. This is what happened to the disciples of the Baptist. Andrew grabbed his brother Simon and told him they had found the Messiah! So Simon follows Andrew and meets Jesus. They wanted to know, *"Where are you staying?"* (John 1:38) Right off the bat, Jesus gives Simon a nickname. He calls him "Rocky." That is what Cephas means, "Rock."

    Nicknames are given to people for various reasons, such as appearance, because of a certain habit, or how they talk, or walk. Me, I was called Peanut, also Peewee, because of my size. I was always very short, and still am. Tough guys were called Rocky. Simon, Andrew's brother, was tough. He had a difficult job. He was a fisherman and that took a great deal of strength to manipulate the nets full of fish, to man the oars in rough seas. Keeping the boats in good repair was very difficult on the hands, forcing pitch and tar into the breeches of wood that had split. Most often, in fact almost always, nicknames are given to people for what they do, who they are at the moment. However, in Simon's case, Jesus gave him the name "Rock" for what he would become, the solid foundation of the Church Jesus intended to build.

    This got me to thinking. What "nickname" would Jesus give to me if He were to appear to me today? Would he call me "Spotty" for all the sinful blemishes on my soul? Would He call me "The Lip" for talking the talk, but not always walking the walk? Would He call me "Sparky" for my quick and volatile temper? Would He call me "Banana Peel" because I keep slipping and falling into sin? Would He call me "The Judge" for my weakness of judging people too quickly? Would He call me "Stranger" because I've been away from Him for too long? Maybe He'd call me "Yo-Yo," for the constant moving away and coming back to Him. OR, would He call me "Old Faithful," "Old Buddy," "Good Servant"? What nickname would I like for Him to tack on me? This a question I seriously need to consider and reflect on.

Andrew brings his brother Peter to Jesus. There are the brief exchanges between Jesus, Andrew, and Peter that, though brief, are very powerful. That's what usually happens when we encounter Jesus; something significant always happens. Jesus turns around and sees them and asks, *"What are you looking for?"* (John 1:38) Jesus could ask that same question of me. Sure, I want to follow Him, but why? What is it I want from the relationship? What am I looking for? Do I follow Jesus because that's what my parents told me I should do? Was it ever a conscious decision on my part to seek out Jesus? Do I still want to be in His presence? I know why I want to follow Him; because He is my Savior, and because of that I love Him deeply. My parents did have a lot to do with my desire to follow Jesus, and I'm very grateful for that formation, but, as an adult, that decision is strictly my own. Now. *What am I looking for?* Am I looking for Him to do great things for me? Do I constantly seek miracles that will make my life easier and more pleasant? I don't think so. I've gotten beyond that. Don't get me wrong. I still pray and petition Him for good health for others and for myself. I pray for good weather for important events. I pray for the poor, the homeless, the jobless, the oppressed, etc., because I know He can make a difference there.

Jesus invites Pete and Andy and us to, *"Come and see."*

Where is He taking us? What is it we will see? What is it He wants us to see? What is it I want to see? After all, God—Father, Son, and Holy Spirit, is spirit and cannot be seen by the human eye. What, then, do we expect to see? After a while, after experiencing this back and forth so many times, we come to realize that what we see, if we care to make the effort, is the presence of Jesus within us. This requires interior vision that, in turn, requires a certain courage, a willingness to look deep within ourselves, beyond the darkness of our human frailty, where resides the image and likeness of our Creator. We see our soul, the one part of us created in His image. What we see is the likeness of God, Himself, as if our soul were a mirror capable of reflecting His image. When we have been purified by His pardon, we can easily see that deep within ourselves, for His light shines so brightly. So brightly does it shine, that we can see Jesus in others, in people we would never suspect, like the homeless, the destitute, the sad, and the sorrowing, even in people whose own light has dimmed for His light can brighten the entire world…if only we would let it. Sounds scary? *Do not be afraid! Come and see!* Come and find out for yourself what Jesus can do. Prepare yourself, though, because once you find out what He's up to, you won't want to let go! Hang on. Trust Him. Trust what you see, what you feel. When it seems that you just can't hang on another minute, call out to Him: *"Jesus, I'm slipping!"* He'll reach right out, snap you up and press you to His bosom so hard, you'll hear His heart beat, the same heart that bled out to save you in the first place. That's where He'll lead you! When you hear Him beckon you, *"Come and see,"* don't be afraid, follow Him to His favorite place to *stay*…your own heart and soul!

But that is not the essence of my relationship with Him anymore. I think what I really seek from Him now is peace and wisdom. I love the good feeling of being close to Him, like a fuzzy warm feeling, a feeling of confidence, a feeling of humble quietness deep within. That is what I seek, because I have felt that way on a few occasions and would like to be that close to Him all the time. Unfortunately, I give in too easy to the distractions of the world, to my own volatile personality, to worldly likes and dislikes. Instead of trying to control all these situations, I have to learn to turn to Him, to trust Him and let Him take control, allow Him to move me around the chessboard of life. That allows me to refocus on what it is I want from Jesus, peace, humility, wisdom, discernment, hope, faith, courage, spiritual fortitude, WHOA! I guess I am asking for a lot! No, not really. You see, when I am really close to Jesus, I get all of that and more. When I allow Him into my life, *like a Good Shepherd He leads me in right paths.* And that leads me to the next chapter.

CHAPTER 5

MY SHEPHERD

Psalm 23

The Lord is my Shepherd, there is nothing I shall want…
He guides me along the right path.

There is no doubting. When we are securely in the flock, under the watchful eye of the Shepherd, it is easy to make decisions that keep us safely encircled in His loving arms. When we listen to His soothing voice, directing us, guiding us, it feels good doing what we are supposed to be doing, pleasing Him, and staying safely within reach of His staff, lest we wander too far astray.

This is a wonderful analogy, but it is flawed. Sheep are not very bright animals, and they are, by nature, followers and stay close to the shepherd not by choice but by instinct. But we, as a people with free will, make choices every day. Unfortunately, we don't always make good ones. We tend to go off on our own, feeling we are intelligent enough to know what we want and need, and how to go about getting both. Sometimes we hear His voice calling us back, and we choose to ignore it. Other times, we are too preoccupied with ourselves to hear Him calling us back. So we drift away. Most of the time, we don't go very far. Our conscience reminds us of how comfortable it is when we are close enough to Him to reach out and hold His hand, especially during difficult times. That is something we have to understand and accept. Though we may be doing everything right and feel very close to God, we will experience difficult times. Being close to God does not make us immune to suffering, to trials and tribulations, nor to pain and suffering, but it does give us someone to dump on, a shoulder to cry on, a strong arm to help us up when we fall and a breath of hope when we feel like we just want to lay down and die.

> *"If I should walk in the valley of darkness no evil would I fear.*
> *You are there with your crook and your staff;*
> *With these you give me comfort."* (PS. 23: 5-6)

The problem is, when we are suffering, when things are going bad, very often we don't want to be around God. We may even blame Him for not being there for us. Believe me, I've been there. I believe it safe to say, we've all been there and are probably there right now. We don't want to pray, and even if we did, we wouldn't know where to begin. Oh, we still believe He can help us, but first He's got to find us, because we sure as hell don't know where we are. That *dark valley of evil* is one scary place. As dark as it is, as evil as it is, there's no place to hide.

Several years ago, I quit smoking, cold turkey. Not a problem. I was a pack and half a day smoker for about twenty years before quitting. I was a non-smoker for about two years when I got the role of Tom in *The Glass Menagerie* by Tennessee Williams. Tom is a chain smoker. My wife was very concerned that I wouldn't be able to give it up again. I reassured her I could and would. I didn't. But I told her I did. Not only was smoking bad for me, my conscience kept reminding me I was lying to my wife and family. I had drifted very far into that *dark valley of evil*. I would begin to pray, asking God to help me quit, but immediately talk myself back into it. I didn't give up on God though; I just didn't want Him butting in at that time. Then things got worse.

One day, my wife came into my office where I was working and caught me red handed. Not only was she disappointed, but let me know it would now be very difficult to trust anything I told her. That really hurt. How could I ever regain that trust? I can honestly tell you it took a very long time. My wife isn't God and couldn't see inside my heart. God knew how sincere I was about never smoking again, but Anna May had no way of seeing that. It would only happen in time, over a long period of time.

He guides me along the right path;
He is true to His name. (PS. 23:3)

How does God do that? How does He guide us? Part of our make-up is something deep within us called a conscience. This is the voice of God. This little, unseen voice begins to develop from the very first "No" we hear as a baby. That is when we begin to learn right from wrong. It takes a few years to develop. Once it does, we soon recognize that uneasy feeling deep within us whenever we do something we are not supposed to be doing. It does take a while to develop to the point where we actually know that we shouldn't do or say something or don't do something when we should. Enter the bane of every conscience: free will. As you can imagine it takes a few years to develop a well-informed conscience, a term that is used for a conscience that excels in discernment. Most of us are well into adulthood before our conscience gets to that point. Discernment is that ability to know whether what your conscience (God) is telling you or not telling you, is the will of God or not. It sounds complicated but it really isn't. Well, maybe just a little. You see, something may be good, like "keeping holy the Sabbath," but if we choose to go to Church on Sunday morning instead of helping out a neighbor who really needs help, that's not so good. Remember the parable of the "Good Samaritan?" So, there are times when we have to make tough decisions. Our conscience is there to guide us, not to dictate to us. We can listen to it or ignore it. Just know that, that is one way God speaks to us. And the volume and power of His voice often depends on how close we are to Him. Our willingness to listen to what our conscience is telling us is also dependent on how immersed we are in the Divine Presence within us.

> *Surely goodness and kindness shall follow me*
> *All the days of my life.*
> *In the Lord's house shall I dwell*
> *For ever and ever.* (PS. 23:6)

Knowing how close or how far we are from God comes from how we feel at any given moment. Yes, the distance between God and us can change in an instant, and becomes very evident by how we feel inside. When we are close to God and doing His will, *goodness and kindness,* follow us and fill the heart with peace and joy. We can be suffering terribly either because of traumatic events in our life or because of physical pain or emotional pain and still feel the goodness and kindness of our Beloved Savior and Creator. I know it sounds silly, but it is an oxymoron of faith. It is spotlighted throughout the Gospels as people seek out Jesus, coming to Him from miles around, traveling through difficult terrain while experiencing great pain and discomfort simply to get a glimpse of Him with the hope of touching His cloak. In Mark 6:56 we read:

> *"...they laid the sick in the marketplaces and begged Him that they might touch only the tassel on His cloak."*

I remember distinctly how His presence within me helped me through a very painful period following back surgery at the beginning of

2003. I had a herniated disc in my lower back. The laminectomy was successful. However, a nerve was stuck on the portion of the disc that had to be removed. In plying the nerve away from the disc, the nerve covering was torn, making it necessary for the surgeon to stitch it back on. I came out of the surgery with the same pain I went in with. It took three months to heal. Besides the physical pain was the worry of not being able to go back to work for three months and not knowing how this would all affect our finances. To borrow a line from Charles Dickens, *"It was the worst of times, it was the best of times."* I was hurting and my range of motion was very limited, but I could pray; I could read and write. It was during that three-month period that the Holy Spirit did some gardening. After my breakfast, I would begin my day by reading the Morning Prayer found in a monthly magazine my wife subscribed to, *The Magnificat*. This little book contained a Morning Prayer, the daily Catholic Mass, a reflection on the Scriptures of the Mass and the Evening Prayer. I found myself writing my own reflection on the Scripture passages chosen for the Liturgy. It was during that period of time that the Holy Spirit planted the idea that I could share these reflections with others by e-mail.

I drew a cartoon character called *Reef Lection* and that became my pen name. The day the first "Reef Lection" was sent out, I had a "typo" in the subject line. I had written <u>God</u> Morning instead of <u>Good</u> Morning. I immediately heard back from a few people who thought that the "subject" was very clever and creative. And that was the start of the "God Morning" group that has grown from a half dozen friends to about fifty people. It has definitely become a ministry, an answer to a call I never would have heard had I not been close to God at the time and reflecting on His Word and what it was saying to me. "God Morning" has also grown to become an occasional prayer line, as some of the recipients will write to me requesting prayers for family members and friends. What the recipients of Reef Lection's writings don't know is that they are more beneficial to me than to anyone else, for they tell me what God is trying to say to me through His Word on a daily basis. And what I don't know is whether or not these reflections work the same way for those who read them. I don't need to know. That's God's job. My job is to give Him something to work with. Something He asked me for. He doesn't ask for much, so who am I to say "No" to Him?

There are many times when I felt that Reef Lection and *God Morning* had run its course, and like Jesus in Mark's Gospel, (7:24), I wanted to go to Tyre for a respite. Every time I start to think in those terms, my conscience raises its voice and reminds me that I'm only doing the typing, that He and His grace are responsible for the words that fill the pages. That is the way with anything we do in His name. He provides the grace, the goodness, and the kindness, and they follow us in whatever, wherever, and whenever we do anything for His praise and glory. Seeking God through pain and suffering, we get close enough to feel the tremendous love He has for us. If only we could stay there. Oh, we can stay, He wants us to stay, but, by our own choosing, we drift away.

CHAPTER 6

LOST SHEEP

Matthew 18: 12-14

"What is your thought on this: A man owns a hundred sheep and one of them wanders away; will he not leave the ninety-nine out on the hills and go in search of the stray? If he succeeds in finding it, believe me he is happier about this one than about the ninety-nine that did not wander away. Just so, it is no part of your heavenly Father's plan that a single one of these little ones shall ever come to grief.

Jesus knows all about us. He has watched His Father play chess with us for years. He also knows we love making our own moves. Sometimes we choose to move closer to Him, the King, sometimes, however, we choose to move away and leave ourselves vulnerable, putting ourselves in peril of getting lost. Matthew describes this situation in his Gospel, chapter 18: 12-14. He tells us Jesus told the crowds a parable. It is the story of a man with 100 sheep and one of them goes off on its own and gets lost. Jesus asks them, *"Will the man not leave the ninety nine on the hillside and go after the one that was lost?"* Of course, we know Jesus was not talking about sheep, but about each one of us. And yes, each one of us has the potential of moving away from Him and getting lost. That is why this teaching of Jesus is so important to us. It reassures us that even though we may lose our sense of what is right, ignoring our conscience and taking the path we want to take, insist on taking, even though it leads to a cliff where we could fall off and be lost forever, Jesus, ever the Good Shepherd, will come after us, seek us, find us, and extend His hand to us, giving us the choice to take His hand and allow Him to pick us up and carry us back in His arms. He comes right out and tells us that when we choose to come back, He is happier with this one that is found than with the ninety-nine who did not wander away. Do not misunderstand. It does not please God when we choose to wander away. What pleases Him is the choice we make to come back. But wander away, we do. Sometimes we get so far away from God it seems that we can't ever find our way back.

Several years ago, I worked at a small radio station with maybe a half dozen people. One of the guys had an office in the back of the building where hardly anyone ever went. It was quiet back there. I often took my own lunch to work and got in the habit of eating in that office while he was on the air and not using the space. One day I discovered a whole stash of pornographic books and magazines. What did I do? I read them, cover to cover. For quite a few weeks I did this until I realized how obsessed I had become with this garbage. The problem was, how do I face God knowing how much I had hurt Him and how far away from Him I had wandered? Do I really believe He forgives me no matter what? Well, I suppose if He can forgive murderers and rapists, He can forgive me. But how do I come back to Him with such darkness inside of me? I was repelled by my own behavior. I was almost convinced He didn't want anything more to do with me as well. Once again, my Christian upbringing and my trust in the Word of God and His grace helped to convince me that Jesus had not abandoned me. He had not given up on me and kept calling out to me. In desperation, I asked for a sign that I would be forgiven. I asked Him to send me a red rose. I was in my car at the time. I had no sooner finished my plaintive plea for forgiveness, than I had to stop for a red light. I looked to the left, and there they were, an entire vine of red roses. I was crying so hard, I had to pull over and dry my eyes so I could see. A mile up the road, I saw a Catholic church, knocked on the rectory door, and when the priest answered the door, I asked to go to confession. He obliged, and I was set free. I can't describe the joy I felt. It's that same joy Jesus says is felt in Heaven when one who has been lost, is found and is the fulfillment of Matthew 18:14 which says,

"Just so, it is no part of your heavenly Father's plan that a single one of these little ones shall ever come to grief."

Most of the time, life isn't that dramatic. Most of the time when we choose to distance ourselves from God, we are not so perilously away from Him, and moving back, sincerely repentant of what we have done, is a lot easier. What is difficult, whatever the distance, is recognizing that we have taken a wrong turn. Many times we try to justify our actions or thoughts and try to convince ourselves that God approves of us 100 percent. That can happen when we misread the signs or misunderstand the voice within us. So, we make a decision on our own, convincing ourselves it is what God has been telling us to do. The next thing you know, we are unhappy and begin to blame God for leading us astray. Well, we all know that God would never do that, so it is time we take inventory. It is time to take a closer look at where we stand and how our life is going. Several years ago, my wife and I worked on a Marriage Encounter team, and the priest that worked with us at the time gave us a standard for knowing whether or not we were doing the will of God. He said that when we do the will of God, there is an unmistakable joy within us, while on the other hand, if it is not the will of God, we will feel stressed, frustrated, uneasy, and unsatisfied with what we are doing. So, when I take that inventory I just mentioned, usually I begin by assessing how I feel. Am I joyful, or am I stressed? So far, that has been a very good measure for me. It quickly lets me know whether I'm moving away from God, or closer to Him. All of this can only happen in response to His grace.

CHAPTER 7

DOUBT & UNBELIEF

Matthew 11: 2-3

Now, John in prison heard about the works Christ was performing, and sent a message by His disciples to ask Him, "Are you the One who is to come, or do we look for another?"

The first three people to recognize Jesus as the promised Messiah were, in order, first, Mary, who agreed to be the mother of Jesus; second, Joseph, who agreed to be His earthly father and third, John the Baptist while still in the womb of his mother, Elizabeth. The angel Gabriel was the messenger who revealed the presence of the Savior to Mary and Joseph, and your guess is as good as mine as to how John the Baptist knew even before seeing the light of day. He leapt in his mother's womb in proclamation of the Divinity within Mary who was visiting her cousin, Elizabeth. That's what being close to Jesus does to us. It moves us, it changes us, it fills us with such joy we want to sing and dance, even while still in the womb! There is no doubt, John was special. At his birth, it was prophesied that He would be the One who would go before the Lord *preparing straight His paths.* (Luke 1:76) In his late twenties and early thirties, John became that prophet and had the privilege of pointing to

Jesus and proclaiming, *"Look, there is the Lamb of God who takes away the sin of the world!"* (John 1:29)

John was a man totally devoted to God and was the product of a miraculous pregnancy. He was dedicated to God at birth and became the greatest of the prophets, having the privilege of seeing the product of his prophecies. He was a man of grace and enlightenment and yet he faltered. He, himself admitted he was not God; he was not the Messiah; he was just the *"the Voice crying out in the wilderness."* His behavior got him arrested by Herod. Up to that point, he had not done anything wrong. But being locked up in a deep, dark dungeon has to weaken even the strongest of spirits. John, who, despite his imprisonment, still had a pretty good following, and was getting reports on what was happening with his cousin, Jesus. Some of what he was hearing had to be a bit disturbing. He was being told that Jesus was saying and doing some very radical things, like; *"In the Kingdom of Heaven, the first shall be last, and the last shall be first." "Whoever wishes to save his life will lose it, but whoever loses his life for my sake and that of the Gospel will save it." "Blessed are the poor in spirit." "To enter into the kingdom of heaven one must be like a little child." "Love your enemies."* That's crazy! And I'm sure John was being told how Jesus was calling the Pharisees names, like *"a brood of vipers"* and *"hypocrites."* That's dangerous! He even healed the daughter of a Centurion. No. Really? John had to be wondering who this Jesus was. Was he really the Holy One of Israel? Had John been misled? Doubt and unbelief began to creep into his soul. In his weakened physical state, his belief system began to get a bit shaky, and ever so slowly, he began to move away from the God of his ancestors. Who to believe, his trusted and loyal followers and friends, or the Holy Spirit, who had enlightened him all his life? He needed to know. Doubt and unbelief got the best of him and so, somehow he got a message to his followers to go and confront Jesus with the question, *"Who are you, really?"*

The reply that Jesus gave echoes down through the ages to this very day for us who might be tormented with doubt or unbelief. Jesus told John's followers,

> *"Go back and report to John what you hear and see: the blind recover their sight, cripples walk, lepers are cured, the deaf hear, dead men are raised to life, and the poor have the good news preached to them."* (Matthew 11:4-5)

That response still resonates with me. I can't confess to unbelief, but doubt? Oh yes. Of course, it all depends on how close I feel to God, whether or not I take daily walks with Jesus and occasional chats in the course of a day and how often my thoughts turn to Him. I have a couple of examples I would like to share with you. Both involve my doubt of being called to a certain ministry and the absolute belief of the ones being ministered to.

I will begin with the story of Jeffrey. This episode begins in September of a year I don't remember, but it was the beginning of the school year. Anna May was volunteering at The Bureau for Exceptional Children and Adults, also known as Jericho. Father Robert F. Wagner founded Jericho in the early 1960s. In the organization's humble beginnings, Father Wagner established religious education classes for people with special needs in some of the larger cities in Western Massachusetts. It was in these classes that people who suffered from mental and physical disabilities received preparation to accept the sacraments of the Catholic Church, a practice most take for granted. Anna May was helping with the Religious Education classes on Wednesday evenings. This group was fairly high-level boys and girls. She came home that first night and asked me if I'd be interested in helping out on Monday night. Monday nights were Religious Ed classes for the less functional boys and girls. Most of them were non-verbal with minimal attention spans. I told Anna May I didn't think I wanted to do that right then. She didn't push. The following week she came back and informed me that they really needed volunteers for Monday nights. Again, I said "No."

Anna May doesn't give up. She returned the following Wednesday with the same request. I knew this would be a weekly thing, and each week adding another *"really"* to they *really, really* need help on Monday nights. So, I said, "Yes," even though I doubted I was being called to do this. I went. I found my role was simply to be a "friend" for about a half an hour to the student they would give me. I got Jeffrey, a tall boy, a truly pleasant kid, but with an attention span of less than five seconds, and a vocabulary of, maybe, ten words. Every movement in the room drew his attention and distracted him from what I was trying to do with him. That was OK with me, since it wasn't vital to the lesson that was planned for the evening. Let me now explain how I really got drawn into Jeffrey's situation. This may seem as a digression—and it is—but is important to this sharing.

Throughout the school year, Fr. Bob, the founder of Jericho, would come in and celebrate Mass before the teaching session. He would do this at the beginning and end of the school year and for the various Holy Days as well. As normal, he would distribute Holy Communion to those who had made their First Communion. When he would come to Jeffrey, Jeffrey would put his hands out to receive the host, but Fr. Bob would pass right by him. Jeffrey would become very sad. I was so touched by the disappointment on his face. After the Mass, I asked Sr. Joan, the assistant director of Jericho and the leader of the Religious Ed classes, why Fr. Bob never gave Jeffrey Communion. She told me matter-of-factly that he had not made his First Communion yet. When I asked why, she told me it was because he could not communicate to her that it was Jesus in the Host. OK. At that moment I was determined to have Jeffrey make his First

Communion. I now had a mission. I brought in pictures of Jesus and tried to get him to tell me who was the man in the picture. All he would tell me was "man." No matter what picture I showed him, the response was the same, "man". I asked Jeffrey his own name and he was quick to tell me, "Jeffrey." So, the "J" sound was there. Jeffrey is not that much different than Jesus. So I kept trying.

It was getting close to Christmas, and I thought, maybe he'll recognize the child in the Christmas scene, so, I brought in a picture of the manger. I pointed to the crib and asked, "Who's that, Jeffrey?"

He answered, "Baby."

Groan. "What's the baby's name?"

"Baby."

I tried a picture with Mary and Joseph around the manger.

"What's the name of Mary and Joseph's baby?"

"Baby."

After Christmas, I went back to pictures of Jesus on the Cross, Jesus kneeling in the Garden, etc. The answer was always the same, "Man." The year ended with a Mass. Jeffrey did not get a Host from Fr. Bob. Jeffrey was disappointed. So was I.

The summer went by and September rolled around. Anna May did not have to beg me to go back. I had no idea what I was going to do, but I knew I had to try. The first day of classes arrived and as usual, Fr. Bob celebrated Mass. The same scenario unfolded with Jeffrey extending his hands to receive communion, and Fr. Bob passing him by.

After Mass, I went over to sit with Jeffrey and, just to make conversation, I asked Jeffrey, "When Fr. Bob celebrates Mass, and hands out the little round Hosts, would you like him to give you one?"

His eyes opened wide and he said, "Yeah, yeah."

Then I asked, "Do you know who is in that little round bread?"

He said, "Yeah, yeah."

Now my eyes opened wide.

"Who?" I asked.

He replied... "Jesus!"

I couldn't believe it. I just couldn't believe it. I think I said, "Right." I immediately went over to Sr. Joan and asked if she had any hosts in her office. She said she had. I asked her to go get one and follow me. On the way to the table, I told Sr. Joan to show the host to Jeffrey and ask him who is in the bread. She gave me a weird, disbelieving look but did, and his answer was most definite, "Jesus." His expression was like, "Why don't you believe me?"

By this time, I was in tears. All this time, Jeffrey had been deprived of the Eucharist because we were asking the wrong question. Needless to say, Jeffrey made his First Communion that year. *Report to him what you hear and see.* Once again, I paid the price for doubting His grace. The price—God smacking me with a two-by-four between the eyes to get my attention. I doubted. He proved to me I shouldn't have. Did I ever do that again? Oh yes!

Several years later, it happened again. And again, the Eucharist was involved. I understand that not everyone believes in the *"real presence"* of Jesus in the Eucharist. It is a belief of Roman Catholics, Eastern Orthodox Catholics, Anglicans, Lutherans and United Methodists. But this story is about my "doubt" in being able to carry out a ministry I was being asked to do and my retreating, moving away from God.

After I retired, I began attending Mass every morning. Soon, our pastoral minister, a nun whom I knew quite well, asked if I would bring Communion to a man who was homebound. I said I would on the condition I didn't have to go into hospitals or nursing homes. She assured me this gentleman lived at home. So I said, "Yes." Then she added another shut-in and another. So far, so good. Then, Archie was added to my list. He had cancer, but lived at home. However, as time went on, Archie had to be hospitalized. I did visit him there. Of course, following a hospital stay he would need therapy. Around here, when seniors need therapy following hospitalization, they end up in nursing homes that provide "*rehab.*" Despite the fact he was placed in one of the worst nursing homes I've ever been in, I went to bring him Communion there. That's when I began to realize that the joy he experienced when he received Communion was worth the sacrifice I had to make to visit him there. Eventually, Archie died, and our pastoral minister retired. Before she could be replaced, our pastor asked me if I would visit the parishioners in two of the local nursing homes. I told him of the agreement I had with Sr. Doris. He didn't blink.

"She's not asking. I'm asking. Will you do it?" was his reply to me. Hmmmm.

"Let me think and pray about it," I said.

A couple of days later, he asked again. I wasn't through praying on it. I just knew I would fail. Well, that would be one way of getting out of that duty.

So, I reluctantly said, "Yes, I'll try it, but don't count on me staying with it, because I really don't think I can handle that." Doubt, with a capital "D".

At this point, let me introduce to you two wonderful women, both in their 80s and both with severe dementia. They are Ethel and Violet. Both had devoted family who visited them every day. Ethel's sister was there in the morning to dress her and feed her and roll her around in a wheelchair all day, meeting and greeting people. Violet's husband was there every day and helped the staff dress her and feed her. Violet did not always recognize her family, and if Ethel did, she, most days, chose to ignore her sister's presence.

Enter, little old me, who really doesn't want to be there, but determined to not let on about my aversion to nursing home facilities and my attitude of failure. Violet was in the first home I went into. She turned out to be the mother of a very good friend of mine. His name is Dennis also. When I introduced myself to Violet, you can only begin to imagine how confusing that had to be to her. After I told her I had Communion for her, her face softened, and she even smiled. I began to pray, and she followed me as best she could. As the weeks went on, as soon as she would see me, her face would light up, and she would attempt to speak but simply couldn't remember how. I asked her son if this was how she greeted her husband when he came. No, it wasn't. Violet recognized her son only occasionally. But she knew me! At first, I thought it was because I was so ugly. Then it dawned on me. It was not me she recognized. It was that little round Host with the real presence of Jesus in it that she recognized. I'm not sure how many years I saw Violet, but I will never forget the last time I saw her. It was the only time I heard her speak. The last few months of her life, I was not able to give her the host, not even a crumb. She had forgotten how to swallow. But I continued to see her every week, and we would say The Lord's Prayer together. I say together. I would recite the words, and her lips would move, reciting that prayer in her mind and heart. Now, the last time I visited her, two or three days before she died, we finished the Lord's Prayer, she looked at me with the clearest eyes and said, clear as a bell, "I love you."

I said, "I love you too."

I hugged her, and then made a quick exit with tears flowing like a river. It was the last time I saw her. She died a few days later.

Then, there was Ethel. Ethel was in a different nursing home, and I met her the same day I met Violet. Ethel was in her mid-eighties and was the oldest of five girls. She had never married, having lost her mother when she was a teenager. She stayed home and took care of her father. Three of her sisters were in nursing homes as well, in other cities. Her youngest sister, Gladys, came to see her every day, from early morning until after dinner. The first time I met Ethel, there was very little response.

Ethel couldn't speak, but would mumble and jumble words. One could usually tell what mood or meaning she intended those words to convey. Gladys had warned me not to expect too much and told me it would be difficult to get her to open her mouth to receive even the tiniest piece of the Host. That was never a problem. By the third week, I was Ethel's best friend, and I was hooked to this ministry. As I mentioned earlier, at first, I thought it was me they were recognizing, but soon it was very obvious it was the *real presence of Christ* in the Eucharist they hungered for. I don't remember exactly when it happened, maybe the third week or the fourth, but that day I walked in the foyer of the nursing home, and Gladys had rolled Ethel there from her room. As soon as Ethel saw me, both her arms went out for a hug. Her sister began sobbing. It was the first time Ethel had hugged anyone in years. Then I got another hug before I left. There was God aiming that two-by-four right between my eyes once again. Doubt was eliminated and without it there, I was able to move, to inch a bit closer to God.

> *"Go back and report to John what you hear and see: the blind recover their sight, cripples walk, lepers are cured, the deaf hear, dead men are raised to life, and the poor have the good news preached to them."*

Whenever I reflect on the things I've heard and seen while bringing the Eucharist to those who can no longer come to church, I feel so ashamed at the doubt I experienced and tremble at how close I came to saying "No" to His grace, that is always sufficient.

    Here's another story of how God helps us overcome our fears and doubts. However it is not my story. It is Anna May's, and I'll let her share it with you.

My mom was widowed the year before Denis and I got married. She had no gainful employment and was trying to manage on an insufficient monthly social security check. I was the youngest of fourteen children, and the last one to "leave the nest." Under the circumstances, it seemed logical to Denis and me that my mom should live with us. It was a decision that many frowned upon, but it turned out to be an incredible blessing to us. I am eternally grateful to Denis for the kind and loving son-in-law he was, and the wonderful care he exhibited in my mom's regard.

Sixteen years into our marriage, my then-elderly mom had a stroke while visiting a sister who lived in another state. Her hospital stay and a short recuperation period lasted about a month before she was able to return home. During that time, my sister and I had a disagreement—she thought my mom should remain there, but my mom wanted to come back to the home she knew and to the area where most of her children resided. Although my sister and I never stopped talking, our relationship became quite strained. My mom died four years later, and my sister moved to Florida. Soon afterwards, my sister had a knee replacement. None of her children were in the area to help, but it was at the time of year when I was off work for the summer. I was experiencing a persistent nagging feeling to go to help her. Yet each time I spoke with her, she rejected my offer.

Then, finally, I simply said, "Do you want me to come to help you?" and to my amazement, she replied, "I would love for you to come and help me."

Now, let me tell you a secret: I fear traveling! Also, I had NEVER traveled ALONE! Yet, there I was, on a train, by my-

self, heading to Florida in response to a "nagging feeling" (the Holy Spirit). And, I wasn't afraid! God definitely accompanied me on that journey. He decided that it was time for my sister and me to be reconciled, and that's exactly what happened during that three-week visit. I am grateful for the gift of God's grace that allowed me to respond to the "nagging" of the Spirit. Praise God; He heals all wounds!

CHAPTER 8

OPEN DOOR

Psalm 25: 4, 8-12

Your ways, O Lord, make known to me; teach me your paths.

Good and upright is the Lord;

Thus He shows sinners the way.

He guides the humble to justice, he teaches the humble His way.

All the paths of the Lord are kindness and constancy toward those who keep his covenant and His decrees.

For your name's sake, O Lord, you will pardon my guilt, great as it is.

When a man fears the Lord, He shows them the way he should choose.

Revelation 3:8

I know your deeds; that is why I have left an open door before you, which no one can close. I know that your strength is limited; yet you have held fast to my word and have not denied my name.

The fact that we, as Christians, move in and out of God's presence, going back and forth like yo-yos has been fairly well established at this point. We move away from God when we give in to temptation, or as the editor of *The Magnificat*, a daily prayer book, put it, *when we fall prey to the ancient whisper of the Garden, "we can become like gods."*

We begin to find our way back to God when we turn around, repent, and begin the slow process of moving closer and closer to God. Moving away from Him seems to be the easy part of the equation. Repenting and finding our way back is a little tougher. In the process of creating an outline for this book, these two passages, made an impression on me. I read them at separate times and made a note to use them. I wasn't sure what they were saying to me at the time, but I felt something about them I can't explain. I was going to use them individually, giving each one its own chapter. When I began this chapter, I started with the reflection on the passage from Revelation. It wasn't developing the way I had intended it to, when a note I had jotted down regarding Psalm 25 caught my attention. I reread the Psalm and was guided into putting the two passages together. They just seemed to go hand-in-hand naturally.

The Psalm seems to assume I have sinned and felt quite removed from the love of God. Scripture scholars tell us that David wrote most of the Psalms, and it would not surprise me to find out that he wrote this one, knowing he had become distant from God by the things he did and didn't do, his thoughts and desires, and his attitudes towards his family, his staff, his subjects and towards God, Himself. These are all things we, too, can be guilty of and so the Psalm speaks to us very pointedly. In this Psalm, we discover ways David saw of working his way back to that *open door.* Revelation 3:8 reveals is there and cannot be closed. First, He *guides the humble to justice.* Humble and Just. I'm not at all surprised that the Palmist lumped them together. I have a lot of trouble with humility, and that is most likely why one of my major weaknesses is judging people.

Judging others is a form of injustice because I do not base my judgments on actual facts, but rather on how a person dresses, or speaks, or by their actions often times even before I know them. That is so unfair, presumptuous, and arrogant on my part. Obviously, these attitudes keep me at arm's length, if not further, from God. As the *Light of the World,* glowing brightly through that *open door* as a guide back to Him, I need to work very hard at acquiring the virtue of humility. As a humble person, there would be no need for me to judge others, except to keep my family and me safe. Yes, there are times when I need to make a judgment for my own safety and that of my loved ones. That is the reason why we all need to pray for discernment so that we can make better and fairer decisions about the people we come in contact with every day. Humility and justice do go hand-in-hand, and they serve us well in getting closer to God and keeping us there.

Next the Psalm says;

> *"All the paths of the Lord are kindness and constancy toward those who keep his covenant and his decrees."*

So, by keeping His Commandments, we keep ourselves open to that constant outpouring of grace that keeps us vigilant and strong against all temptation. It is through the kindness of our Lord that His grace is always there, and as we know, His grace is sufficient. There isn't anything we can't do when we do it in His name. He can ask anything of us and we should not be afraid. *"Be not afraid; do not fear."* I'm not a bean counter, but I am going to say that this is the most quoted phrase in all of Holy Scripture, uttered by Angels, Prophets, God the Father and Jesus. After Jesus ascended into heaven, I'm sure His Apostles and disciples calmed their listeners and followers with the same, *"Do not be afraid."* In documented apparitions throughout the centuries, Mary, the Mother of Jesus, spoke those same words. Yet, so often, when we are being led to take on a task we have never done before, we are nervous, suspicious, and downright scared. So many times, I have said to the person asking me to help with something, "I'll do this for you, my friend." I've had it said to me, as well. NO. NO. When God calls us, either by speaking directly to our heart, or through someone else, say, *"YES, Lord, I'll do it for you and in your name."* Don't do it for a friend. And the friend is not asking for himself, anyway. God asks us to work for Him because we are righteous people who *"keep His commands and decrees."* We, in turn should say *"yes"* because we know He is kind and generous and constant with His grace, providing the strength, knowledge, and courage to do His will, to stay on that *path* that leads closer and closer to Him.

Next, the Psalm says;

"For your name's sake, O Lord, you will pardon my guilt, great as it is."

Forgiveness. When we are walking down the path that leads away from God, forgiveness is that grace that turns us around and puts us back on the right path that leads back to Him, to that *open door that will never be closed.* Forgiveness, something we should readily give; something we should not be afraid to ask for. There is no greater feeling than being forgiven. It is freeing, exhilarating. I don't understand why Catholics are so afraid to partake in the Sacrament of Reconciliation. Coming away from it, pardoned of your transgressions, forgiven, is an incredibly joyous moment. The entire world seems lifted from your heart and shoulders. It's freedom, freedom from guilt, not responsibility, but guilt. Often, forgiveness requires reparation for the offense because many times our transgressions injure and harm others who need consolation from us. Fulfilling that responsibility also puts us back on the pathway that leads to the heart of Jesus. Forgiveness, whether forgiving or being forgiven, is a warm, loving embrace from God.

Finally the Psalm tells us;

> *"When a man fears the Lord, He shows them the way he should choose."*

In recent times the phrase, *"fear of the Lord,"* has been translated into *"reverence of the Lord."* I like that better, yet there is still something inside me that tells me that *fearing* the Lord is not a bad thing. When we do something to offend Him, punishment should follow. That's what responsible parents do. So, yes, I feel we should fear the power that He has to exact severe punishment. On the other hand, *fear* is not the best reason for leading a righteous life. Love is the best reason. Whether we do something out of love for God, or to revere Him, or because we fear Him it is far better than ignoring Him, or turning our backs on Him. When we do listen to Him and follow His Commandments and decrees, and do so out of reverence for His name and for who He is, He will continue to show us the way we should choose. We will continue to be in full view of that *open door, His Sacred heart,* through which the *Light of the World* shines brightly, guiding our every step. Pope Benedict XVI once wrote:

> *His divine heart calls to our hearts, inviting us to come out of ourselves, to abandon our human certainties to trust in Him and, following His example, to make of ourselves a gift of love without reserve.*

We must not be afraid of taking the steps necessary that move us closer and closer to Him. We should heed the advice of St. Pius of Pietrelcina, who was an Italian Capuchin priest who said:

"When you are unable to take big steps on the path that leads to God, be content with little steps, patiently waiting until you have the legs to run."

I would like to comment on that *open door* that has been left opened for us. One night, while lying in bed waiting to go to sleep, I began thinking about this *open door.* I began thinking of it as the heart of Jesus. When I am really close to God, that's where I feel I am, in the heart of God, and that is where He wants me to be. Then my thoughts went one step further. I saw the *open door* as the pierced heart of Jesus on the Cross and the blood and water that came out of the *opened heart* as the water of our Baptism and the blood of our Salvation, and it was as if I heard the centurion saying at that moment, *"Truly, this is the Son of God."* Is the opened heart of Jesus, the *opened door that cannot be closed?* Is it any wonder then that we strive so hard to enter that door and do our best to stay there?

As I think about that, I ask myself, *"Where do I stand with God?"* I need to ask that question quite often. Unfortunately, that is not a good thing. You see, when I am close to God, I know where I stand. I know because of how I feel, how my heart feels. There is a certain joy that is unmistakable. Once you have felt it, you will always recognize it. You just know. It is there whether you are in the most serious difficulty, or the most intense pain. Closeness to God overrides all of that. It is when I don't feel that unmistakable joy that I must ask, *"Where do I stand? How far away from Him am I? What is it that is creating this space between us?"*

Through the Death and Resurrection of Jesus, the door to Him has been opened, and it is a door *no one can close.* I am free to come and go as I please. That is the crux of the problem. I am free to choose, to control my own destiny. I can choose to respond to His grace and therefore act, speak, and think in a fashion pleasing to Him, or not. Because He *knows my deeds*, in fact, He knows everything there is to know about me and thus knows where I stand with Him, He knows when I am close to Him and when I am distant. When I am not close to Him, when I have moved away, He is sad and hurt. He continuously calls to me to bring me back. How does He do that? First of all, there is His Word, Holy Scripture. Then of course there is family, friends, and any number of holy people who offer good advice when they see I am uneasy or unhappy with the way my life is going. Then there is the Church with its Seasons, Rites and Rituals, Liturgies and teachings. One great example is the season of Lent.

At the onset of the Lenten season most of us decide what sacrifices to make for the next six weeks. That's great. Some give up candy, or desserts, some give up their favorite foods or beverages; some put aside a dollar or two a day for the Missions, and some people simply stick to their diets. These are all good things, but are they in the true spirit of Lent? What is Lent and why is Lent? Lent is basically a forty-day period of sacrifice on our part. Why? Why does the Church impose this time of fast and abstinence and sacrifice upon us? Well, to get right down to it, it comes back to one of my favorite sayings; *"When I feel distant from God, who moved?"* One might ask, *"How far away from God could I possibly be? We just had Christmas!"* Oh Yes, Christmas. How much was Christ a part of your Christmas? That *"holly jolly season"* could be the beginning of a gradual slide away from God and into a world of material possessions. Then there are winter, the severity of the weather, and the absence of daylight that can bring about a bit of depression, bad colds, the flu, and all kinds of dreary attitudes, such as *"Where's God in all of this?"* Right where He always is, waiting for you to come back to Him; waiting for you to get bored with all the stuff you got at Christmas and weary from shoveling snow and treating icy sidewalks, filling oil tanks and asking yourself, *"Is that all there is?"* No. That's not all there is.

Turn around. Look behind you. God is waiting for you with open arms. The Lenten season is a season of repentance, of *"turning around."* Most of us have learned that over the years, but one thing we often forget is that Lent is not just a forty-day crash course of going without stuff. If nothing else, let us come to realize that Lent should be a turning back to how God wants us to live every day of our lives, not just for six weeks, from Ash Wednesday to Easter. As we turn around and work our way back to God, however way we do that, should become permanent life changes. Read this passage from Isaiah, chapter 58: 1-9. *(Go ahead, read it. I'll wait.)* God is talking to Isaiah, complaining, actually. He's telling the prophet to go back to His people and let them know He is ticked off with them, because they are nothing more than a bunch of self-centered show-offs. They fast and offer burnt offerings to make themselves look good while they drive their laborers and quarrel and fight with everyone. Then God tells Isaiah exactly the kind of sacrifice He wants. As we read what God wants it should dawn on us, that these are not sacrifices, these actions should be a part of our everyday thinking and attitudes toward our family and our neighbors…and towards Him! These are traits we need to incorporate into the fiber of our lives. We need to stop looking out for ourselves and begin feeling love and compassion for the guy next door. God gives His list to Isaiah to bring to us;

> *"Acting justly; freeing the oppressed; sharing your bread with the hungry; sheltering the homeless; clothing the naked (give a coat to someone wearing only a sweater in zero-degree weather) and don't turn your back on your own."* (Isaiah 58: 6-7)

God knows what He wants, so, I think it might be a good idea to give it to Him. And, when Lent rolls around again, we'll not be asking ourselves, *"What can I give up?"* But, *"What else can I do in your name, Lord?"*

We won't be perfect, but we will be holier and closer to God than ever before. That's what Lent is meant to be, a beacon that lights up the path that leads back to the heart of Jesus, that *open door that cannot be closed.*

Chapter 9

Wealth & Comfort

Mark 10: 17-23

As he was setting out on a journey a man came running up, knelt down before him and asked, "Good Teacher, what must I do to share in everlasting life?"

Jesus replied, "You know the commandments:
'You shall not kill;
You shall not commit adultery;
You shall not steal;
You shall not bear false witness;
You shall not defraud;
Honor your father and your mother.'"

He replied, "Teacher I have kept all these since my childhood." Then Jesus looked at him with love and told him, "There is one more thing you must do. Go and sell what you have and give to the poor; you will then have treasure in heaven. After that, come and follow me." At that, the man's face fell. He went away sad for he had many possessions.

God knew what He was doing when He put His Son Jesus in a human body. This encounter with a rich young man is so tender, yet tough in a good sense. I really feel sorry for the guy because I am that guy. I come running up to Jesus, and He *looks at me tenderly and loves me.* (Mark 10:21) How good is that? Yes, He loves me with all my warts and scales, faults and failures, and the deformities of my many sins. But because I try and do my best, He loves me. Because I am willing to *run* to Him, to seek Him, to find Him, He loves me. Many times, I, too, walk away sad because what He wants of me, I find too difficult. I am afraid to fail yet again. Let me say this, not as a boast, but more as a testament to His grace; as I get older, I realize that what He asks of me is not so scary, is not impossible at all because I have come to know, to believe and to trust that He will walk with me in whatever He asks me to do in His name. The more that I agree to work with Him, the more I realize that what He asks is not to move mountains, because that is what He does. He just wants me to be me; to be helpful, thoughtful, kind, loving, happy, and cheerful, and He wants me to bring Him along to meet and greet the people I meet and greet every day. He just wants me to allow Him to reside within me in order to be visible to the world He created and the creatures He gives life to. Now is that so hard? If you're me, it is. Because in order to do that, I must resist sin, all sin, big and small. When I choose worldly things, He graciously bows out and lets me do my thing and patiently waits for me to come running back. I can't say I come back running, because I'm usually sad and ashamed for turning my back on Him and pushing Him aside to indulge in my own selfish wants and desires. Crawling back would be more like it.

Now, I'm not a "*rich*" man like the man in the Gospel, but I am not poor and destitute either. I have "*things*"; possessions that would be very difficult for me to give up, like my TV for example. It is not one of those theatre sized TVs with surround sound, and all the bells and whistles, and I don't have the top of the line cable package, but I enjoy it, maybe a little too much. I love to play golf and that would be very difficult for me to give up. As I get older, I realize there will come a time when I won't be able to play, physically as well as financially, but so far, He has kept me healthy enough to be able to play. Should He ask me to stop, could I? I would like to think I could and would say, "Yes," to Him. If I was ill and hurting and could no longer swing a club, it would be easier to say, "Yes." However, I know that is not how God works, and some day, He might just ask me to stop playing. Saying "No" would be the same as the young man's response in the Gospel and I would be turning my back on Jesus, walking away sadly, and I'm not sure if I would do that. Then there's other stuff, like this computer, and the Boze I'm listening to, and this warm and comfortable house with nice stuff in it. Again, it's not the best stuff, but it is nice stuff and it is my stuff. I have to admit it is stuff that distracts me from honest, sincere, devout prayer and other spiritual exercises. They are like knots in the string of the yo-yo that keep it from going all the way up and into the hand and heart of God. Knowing that, I still don't get rid of this stuff. I justify it by saying, *"God has blessed me with a good life and a good family and it would be sinful to reject these blessings."* In a sense this is true, but it is a cop-out. One thing I can honestly say is that I regard my stuff as just that, stuff, and it never takes precedence over people, family, or God. If I lose them, I know I can live without them, yes, even my golf clubs, or my ability to use them. I know that giving up things that give me pleasure is a difficult issue because as I sit here writing this, I am at a time in my life when I am going to have to rid myself of much of what surrounds me, because we are looking at downsizing in order to get into smaller, more manageable living space.

    Lately, whenever I read this Gospel passage, I can truly identify with the *"rich young man"* and choose to walk away sad, and I'm certain Jesus is sad as well. Any time I choose something or someone in preference to Jesus, the Father, or the Holy Spirit, it saddens the God that loves me unconditionally, and so often that is the choice I make.

I remember when we were kids, during the Lenten season my Mom and Dad would gather us around the kitchen table after the dinner dishes were washed and put away, and we would recite the Rosary. When my wife was a child, her mother gathered all her kids for the Rosary every night, not only during Lent. As I got older, we stopped doing that. Why? I have no idea. Not that we were bad. We simply chose to do something else with that time, and it wasn't prayer. I bring the Holy Eucharist to people in the nursing home. On many occasions, I see people making the Sign of the Cross and whispering the "Our Father" with me, then looking with tear filled eyes as I give the Eucharist to the people from my parish. I always ask if there are others who would like to receive. Now and then the response is, *"Yes, but I left the Church years ago."*

My response to that is; "Do you believe in the real presence of Jesus in the host?"

If the answer is "Yes," I give them Communion. It is not for me to judge why they walked away, and I feel I have just welcomed them back.

One of the most difficult tasks I've ever taken on is promoting men's weekend retreats. Generally the weekend retreat begins on Friday evening and ends Sunday noon, following the Sunday Liturgy. It isn't an excessive amount of time. Most retreat centers are located in quiet suburban areas and offer very peaceful surroundings. The format of retreats vary, but most offer inspiring talks from a team of three or four, priests and laymen, morning and evening prayer, a liturgy, and plenty of time for soul searching. Doesn't that sound wonderful, a weekend away from all the hubbub and responsibilities, with plenty of time to work on one's relationship with God with the goal of growing closer to Him? Ask any man who attends church services regularly, and he will agree that a retreat is a wonderful idea. Then ask if you can sign him up for the next retreat. Oh boy! You will be amazed at all the different excuses you will hear. Like the rich young man in the Gospel, they walk away sadly, spouting off a litany of excuses; "I would like to go, but..."

Time, of course, is the number one reason they give for not being able to go. I've heard some dandies.

One fellow said to me, "A retreat? That's too much holy stuff for me."

I replied, "You are planning on going to Heaven when you die, right? Well, I got news for you. That's a lot more holy stuff than a retreat."

He thought I was a wise guy and walked away. Sad. Even sadder was the man who approached me after I had made a plea to the congregation following the Sunday service. He was with his wife, and I could see that he wanted to go, but they looked at each other and finally agreed, "Right then was not a good time."

I felt it was a financial situation and explained the policy of the Retreat Center we attend, *"Give more if you can and less of you can't."* They don't want the cost of the weekend to be a barrier for any individual. Despite my explanation, the man chose not to go, to walk away from the opportunity to get a little closer to Jesus. Two months later, the man died suddenly at the age of fifty.

Every year, our pastor allows me to speak to the congregation after all the Sunday services about a month before the parish's scheduled weekend retreat. I don't know how many men there are in our parish, but I'd guess it's well over 500. The average number of men who attend the retreat is between eight to twelve. Sad. What is it that makes them turn away from the opportunity to *follow* Jesus and spend some quality time with Him? Hopefully they are finding other ways to respond to the call to follow Jesus, a way that is more comfortable for them and more suited to their spirituality. Again, we are not bad people. We simply have too many options to choose from. Some of them are legitimate, like spending time with family. In today's economy, Mom and Dad both need to work, and weekends are their only time together. I get that, and applaud the parents who choose to give their children as much of themselves as they can. The danger there, is that the choices we, as parents, make are the choices our children will make when they become adults. In the course of our lives, our children have to see us making good decisions, decisions that include responding to the voice of Jesus offering us to *"follow Him."* The closer we can get to Jesus, the clearer His voice will be, and the more likely we will respond with a "Yes." And, of course, the more often we do that, the more we will come to understand that whenever He calls us to *follow* Him, His grace is there to give us the strength and courage we need for the journey. And by all means, bring the children with you. Jesus' love for children is legend!

This seemed like a very good place to end this chapter, but I have one more suggestion to make. Whenever life seems to be ganging up on you; when you know you are doing everything right, but you find yourself asking, "Is this all there is?" whenever you feel dissatisfied with the way life is treating you; when you're down in the dumps and feel that God is out there somewhere and only God, Himself, knows where, ask yourself, "Who moved?" Then, when you realize that it isn't God who moved, take a good, honest look at the things and activities you place ahead of God. Ask yourself what do you do, where do you go, how do you prefer to spend your time when given the opportunity to pray, to meditate, or to roll up your sleeves and help Him do some of His work. Be honest. Be not afraid. Don't be shy. He loves having us close to Him. There's nothing that gives Him more pleasure than having you close enough so He can wrap you up in His arms.

Having said that, I must tell you that I have always admired the Apostles and disciples of Jesus who gave up everything, job, home, family and friends to follow Him and often wondered if I would have done that. I am sure there was something very compelling about Jesus that inspired them and filled them with the courage it took to trust this itinerant preacher. Was it His appearance, something in His eyes? Was it His voice? There had to be something that set their hearts on fire and made them drop everything when He said, *"Come, follow me."* That compelling component, I believe, is called grace, the same grace that compels me when He calls me back after having fallen away from Him. Every time I am touched by His grace and repent and come back to Him, *"He looks at me and loves me."* (Mark 10:21) Is it any wonder then that I know I am His Beloved, one of His disciples. And that's how He is with each and every one of us!

CHAPTER 10

ROCK BOTTOM

Micah 6:8

You have been told what is good and what the Lord requires of you; only this, to act justly, to love tenderly and to walk humbly with your God.

Psalm 42: 3-4

Athirst is my soul for God, the living God.
When shall I go and behold the face of God?

My tears are my food day and night,
As they say to me day after day, "Where is your God?"

Mark 8: 11-13

The Pharisees came forward and began to argue with Him. They were looking for some heavenly sign from Him as a test. With a sigh from the depth of His spirit He said, "Why does this age seek a sign? I assure you, no such sign will be given it." Then He left them, got into the boat and went off to the other shore.

But Jesus invades all those places, and thereby illumines them. He offers us new life even when we've wandered as far as we possibly can from God.

In that sense, the Cross was necessary for our salvation since it allowed the Hound of Heaven to hunt us down, even in the darkest places.

– Fr. Robert Barron

Using superlatives is a very risky business, so I will not say that everyone hits rock bottom at some time or other. I am going to assume, however, that most people do. I have, a few times, and I can attest to the fact, to a couple of facts, actually. The first one is that it is about as rotten as I've ever felt in my life. The second fact is that some mystical factor invades every fiber of my being, screaming, *"DO SOMETHING!"* It's not a scream of fear and probably is the wrong word for it. It is a strong voice, an insistent voice urging me to get rid of the *"poor me"* attitude and start looking for something positive, for something to be hopeful about. When you feel there is no hope ever of your getting out of the funk you're in, of ever feeling better, of ever being of any value, of ever having someone love you and care what happens to you, you tend to tune out that mystical voice, because it's coming from such a far away, empty place. You somehow know it is the voice of God but you don't care. You have drifted so far from God, you have become so removed, you feel totally abandoned. You just want to roll over and die. But then, something strange happens. You don't know it at the time, or are unwilling to admit it, but God's grace, like a flickering candle in a deep cave sparks a glimmer of hope. Fr. Robert Barron says it best:

> *"But Jesus invades all those places, and thereby illumines them. He offers us new life even when we've wandered as far as we possibly can from God.*
>
> *In that sense, the Cross was necessary for our salvation since it allowed the Hound of Heaven to hunt us down, even in the darkest places."*

You begin to hear things, like, *I'm praying for you." "God never forgets or abandons you." "Put your trust in Jesus, He knows what you're going through."* How would He know? Suddenly the words of the Creed come to you; "*He died and descended into hell…"* He does know! You begin to pray, just a little at first, and begin reading the Bible, just a little. You might even start with a favorite Psalm. For future reference make a note of this one, Psalm 42: 3-4. Yes, my soul is thirsty for God, but where is He? It's a beginning and slowly but surely you find yourself returning to normal. You begin looking for signs to give yourself reasons to trust, to hope. *"Show me a sign, Lord, that you are there, that you see my pain. "I need to know that everything will be OK."* Every now and again you hear an answer; *"Isn't my Word enough for you?* What does that mean? Then one day you're sitting in church, and you hear the Gospel being proclaimed from the pulpit. It's Mark 8: 11-13.

> *"They were looking for some heavenly sign from Him as a test."*

You ask yourself, "Why do I need more signs? Look at all the things He's already done for me." And that's when you realize how far away from God you had moved. Yes, YOU had moved; not Him.

I would like to believe that your life is not much different from mine. Maybe in details, but not in general; there are good times and bad times; happy times and sad times. We give, we take; we're up, we're down. And through it all, God is right there caring for us, working miracles for us, some big, some small, but miracles nonetheless; "signs" if you will. Let me tell you about our fifth child, our daughter Laurie. It's a long story, so get comfortable and fasten your seat belts. It is because of her, I don't believe in miracles anymore…I depend on them!

Laurie, our fifth child was born in 1967, during the seventh year of our marriage. It was a different pregnancy, somewhat difficult for Anna May, and there were times when we wondered if she would carry the baby through. But she made it full term. The delivery was very different also, and in fact, we almost lost Anna May. Fortunately, the doctor and the nurses acted swiftly and competently, and both Anna May and the baby, a girl, made it safely through the ordeal. We named her Laurie, a derivative of Elizabeth, meaning consecrated to God. Little did we know at the time that would actually happen.

Laurie seemed to progress a little slower in her first year of life than her siblings. Right about the time she would celebrate year one, Anna May and I noticed some mild twitching of her head and arms. We immediately told her pediatrician, who, after examining her, sent us to a neurologist. At that time there were no pediatric neurologists anywhere near where we lived. Various medications were tried but the "little" seizures persisted. The doctor did give them a name, "myoclonic" seizures. It did not make us feel any better. The neurologist guessed at the cause, *brain damage that occurred at birth.* *"Seizures." "Brain damage."* These are serious words. They are very difficult words to digest when they are applied to your baby girl. I don't remember exactly how I felt when the doctor spoke them, but I do know it wasn't good.

At that time, I know I wasn't all that close to God. I would go to church on Sunday, and that was the extent of my spirituality. I do know I did not blame God for our daughter's physical condition. I wasn't even sure what her physical condition was. My wife and I did pray a lot, not knowing what was going to happen. Would she get worse? Was there a cure? Would they be able to control the seizures? Would she be capable of learning? We were young and had no idea what to expect. Our other four children were all healthy and bright. We had no idea what was in store for us. We had no idea how much we would have to depend on God. We had no idea how close to God we would become in the years ahead, all because of Laurie and the miracles He would work in her precious life.

In the first four years of Laurie's life, it became very evident that the *"brain damage"* definitely caused learning disabilities as well as physical limitations. Her vocabulary consisted of about twelve words, and she was very unsteady on her feet. The seizures were still not under control. The neurologist decided to address the speech problem and suggested we take her for speech therapy. Although we didn't know it at the time, the best speech therapist in New England was right here in our city. Thus began God's first little miracle, but as usual, it wasn't exactly what we expected nor did it happen when we expected it. In fact, it wasn't until a few years later that we realized what God had done. Allow me to digress for a moment.

Anna May, being the youngest of fourteen children, immersed us in a loving family that was very supportive and caring, especially her brother Charlie. Charlie's birth date is July 26. That is the feast day of Ste. Anne. Ste. Anne is the grandmother of Jesus. There is a huge Basilica in Beaupre, Canada, dedicated to Ste. Anne that is world renowned for all kinds of miraculous healings. Charlie kept insisting that we take Laurie there.

"You take her there and Laurie will talk," he told Anna May on several occasions.

Ste. Anne de Beaupre was 450 miles from our home, which meant at least one overnight in a motel. Money was very tight back then, but we were desperate. So, as nervous and fearful as we were about the trip, we decided to give it a go. The summer before Laurie turned four years old, we packed the five kids and my mother-in-law into our little Buick Special and headed for Canada, about a nine-hour trip back then. We visited the Shrine at Ste. Anne de Beaupre, prayed, attended the services and liturgies, and headed back home the next day. No big, instant miracle.

But I believe Ste. Anne got her Grandson's attention.

Back to the speech clinic. After five or six weeks, Mrs. Ezat, the director of the clinic called us in her office. She told us what we expected to hear, and it was refreshing to finally have someone, especially a professional person, agree with us. Laurie did not have a speech problem, she had a language problem. Here's where God enters the picture. Mrs. Ezat handed us a business card. The card belonged to the director of the Children's Language Institute in Ludlow, MA, just a few miles from our home. This school was founded by a husband and wife who were schoolteachers and whose daughter was also Aphasic, a language disorder. They used all their savings and mortgaged their home to start the Institute, which opened its doors just three months prior, in September 1971. Laurie was evaluated and began attending the school in January. Within two months, Laurie's vocabulary expanded by another 25 words. Soon she was speaking in two- or three-word sentences. It was amazing. We still didn't connect the dots yet between Ste. Anne de Beaupre and Laurie's wonderful progress. We just thought it was due to professional schooling. Her seizures were not under control and various medications and dosages were tried with very little success, and she still had a very stilted walk and poor hand coordination.

At age seven, Laurie's progress in school hit a plateau. Her teachers asked if they could see the reports from her neurologist. We signed the release forms and brought them to the doctor. The doctor did not send the information, although she said she would. After several phone calls and still no cooperation, her pediatrician sent us to another neurologist. Two visits later we were done with him, too. Our pediatrician then set up an appointment for Laurie at Children's Hospital in Boston. God was working His little miracles, playing chess with us. We were very nervous about going to Boston for medical care, even though we knew that Boston was the Mecca of medicine. But this was for our daughter, so we said a few prayers and headed down the Mass Pike. If I had a dollar for every trip we have made on that highway since then, I'd be a wealthy individual. Anyway, we kept the appointment at Children's Hospital, and within a few brief hours, we had a diagnosis and a prognosis. We were part of every exam they performed. Laurie was never separated from us.

When they were satisfied that they had found the problem, the doctor sat us down and explained, *"Laurie has a genetic condition causing a mild to moderate case of Tuberous Sclerosis. Because of that, her body has already produced some tumors. Some are located in her brain causing the difficulty with language and the seizures."*

The prognosis was that, as Laurie got older, tumors might develop on various organs, some might be removed by surgery while others might not. This time, I remember how I felt. I was scared. I felt helpless. I was totally confused. I had never heard of Tuberous Sclerosis. Just as I was about to ask, the doctors told us they didn't know all that much about the condition because, though not a rare one, it was not that common. Because it was a genetic disorder, we would be interviewed and maybe even tested to see if one of us had passed it down to her. It turned out, we didn't, and that it was what is called a *"spontaneous mutation."* I still didn't feel any better, but neither I nor Anna May blamed God for this or asked *"Why us? Why Laurie?"* We never blamed Ste. Anne for not healing our daughter. In fact, we felt it was the hand of God that led us to Boston. We finally had an answer to Laurie's medical problem. The doctors there cooperated with her school, and once more, Laurie was making progress.

As time went along, the idea of inoperable tumors were put in the back vault of our memory bank. Laurie was speaking in full sentences, doing easy math, her gross motor nerve problems were corrected, and she was developing excellent athletic skills. We were now convinced that Ste. Anne had definitely got Jesus' attention, and although Laurie's condition still existed, it was obvious, Laurie was educable. Our spiritual life had improved drastically through prayer and through Holy Scripture. As a couple and as individuals, we had definitely begun moving closer to God and found so much comfort in His presence.

Then, Laurie hit puberty, and once again things changed drastically. Laurie's seizures were pretty much under control, but not entirely. One day, Laurie was playing on the floor with her older sister, Lisa. Suddenly, Lisa said, *"Mom, I think Laurie is having a seizure."* Sure enough, but this one was very different. It was a grand mal seizure and lasted about 30 seconds. During the next year or so, Laurie had five more. Again, the doctors at Children's Hospital were puzzled. One day, Anna May decided it was time to make another visit to Ste. Anne de Beaupre. On this particular visit, something definitely happened. The Basilica is huge, as you can imagine. Between the pews and the sanctuary on the left side is a very large statue of Ste. Anne. As we stood in front of the statue, Anna May explained to Laurie the relationship between Anne and Jesus. Laurie was very familiar with grandmothers, since Anna May's mom lived us from the time we were married. Prior to her death, she would play various games with Laurie after school. When Anna May finished her explanation, Laurie became quiet for a good minute or two, then with a shake of her head, as if coming out of a trance, she came over to us, and we proceeded to leave the Basilica. The Basilica sits up high, and there are quite a few stairs to descend to the ground level.

At the top of the stairs, Laurie stopped dead I her tracks and said, *"I feel so good inside."*

We were stunned. Laurie had never expressed a feeling before. Feelings are abstracts, something Laurie could not grasp for a long time. But even better than that, Laurie never had another seizure. She was fourteen at the time and is now in her late forties. It never dawned on us until at age twenty Laurie was badly in need of orthodontic work, but the dentist couldn't do anything because her gums were so soft due to her seizure medication. We approached her neurologist, who checked her chart and noticed Laurie had been seizure free for about seven years. Instead of changing the meds, she suggested we take Laurie off seizure meds completely. We agreed. Still no seizures. Her present neurologist, who is the director of the Carol and James Herscot Center for Children and Adults with TSC (Tuberous Sclerosis Complex) at Mass General Hospital, does not admit that it is miraculous, but doesn't say it isn't either. She does admit that it is very rare that TSC patients become seizure free without medication. I'm convinced it's the hand of God. Oh, there's more. I'm just getting started, but I do want you all to know that Anna May and I have never prayed for a cure. Our prayer has always been, *"Lord, she's in your hands. You take care of her according to your will, and give her and us the grace to accept that."* We never asked for signs. Oh, I do admit it would have been nice if the TSC would have just disappeared. But it didn't.

However, Ste. Anne's Grandson wasn't done with her yet. He was taking good care of her. He had a hand in her schooling. As one door would close, another would open. We had to fight for the right education, and fight we did. Again, God was playing chess and put the right people in the right places, including us, at just the right time. The frosting on the Educational Cake is that Laurie got a job before she graduated from high school. The same job she holds today. How did that happen? God took Anna May away from high stress legal secretarial work, and got her a job at Mt. Holyoke College. A few years later, the college hired Laurie as Anna May's assistant. That was over 25 years ago, and though Anna May is retired, Laurie is still there. That's not really a huge miracle, but the reality is that very few Special Ed people get jobs for which they were trained. I classify it as one of His little miracles.

Now back to Laurie's health issues. After the seizures stopped at age fourteen, Laurie's health didn't seem to be much of a problem. We had totally forgotten about the prognosis given to us at Children's Hospital when Laurie was seven years old. We had forgotten about the possibility of tumors growing and affecting vital organs. Laurie was very active, a good athlete, winning Gold Medals in the Special Olympics. She rarely missed a day of work, and orthodontics had given her a winning smile. Then one day when I went to pick her up after work (she works only four hours, 8-12), Laurie wasn't coming out of the office. I waited awhile. After about 10 minutes, I went to the office to see what was keeping her. I found her, lying on the floor in excruciating pain. Thinking it was appendicitis, we rushed her to the local hospital. They immediately ran a blood test, but her white blood cell count was good, and they ruled out appendicitis. They kept her overnight, and first thing the next morning, they performed an ultrasound. Fortunately, Anna May was there as her legal guardian. The technicians were having trouble reading what they were seeing and kept asking Laurie if she was sick. Laurie answered "No," but she was in pain. Then Anna May realized what they were asking and told the technicians she had Tuberous Sclerosis. Once again, the bottom was about to fall out. It was then we found out that Laurie's kidneys were full of tumors and that one of them had an aneurism that was leaking blood into her stomach cavity, causing the pain. Now what? What do we do now? Where do we go? Her neurologist was at the Lahey Clinic in Burlington, MA just outside of Boston. We knew that the local doctors had no experience with Tuberous Sclerosis patients. But who did? We soon found out. Again, not really a big miracle by most standards, but in my opinion, this was a biggie.

Over the years, about every other month, we would receive a newsletter from a TSC group with information about research and information that was coming to light through the experiences of patients willing to share their story. Anna May kept every issue. I had no idea she was saving those. She remembered that in one of the issues, they addressed the problem of renal tumors. While she was going through these newsletters looking for that one issue, she found one that listed all the TSC clinics in the country. Lo and behold, there was a TSC clinic at Mass General Hospital in Boston. We immediately contacted them and got an appointment with the neurologist heading up the clinic, who then set up an appointment for Laurie with a urologist. Six months later, that urologist put together a team of nuclear medicine surgeons that saved Laurie's life when the aneurism burst. The fact that she was already in the Emergency Room at Mass General Hospital when the aneurism burst was a miracle in itself. The tumor had begun bleeding again and, following her MGH doctor's advice, we brought her into the local hospital. All they did was give pain medication and sent her home. They did this twice. After the second time, Anna May suggested we pack a bag and head to Boston. Most people would not consider that a miracle. But had we waited till morning to call the local doctor, Laurie would have bled to death during the night. What motivated us to pack a suitcase and head for Boston at 9 o'clock at night? It was certainly the grace of God, giving us the insight and the courage. Ste. Anne's Grandson taking charge! Now remember, we didn't ask for these miracles, but more and more, we began depending on them. A few years later we got another big one.

The aneurism that burst was in Laurie's right kidney. From that point on, her urologist would order an ultrasound once a year. A few years after losing a part of her right kidney the ultrasound detected what looked like a black tumor in her left kidney. They immediately did a biopsy, and it came back positive for cancer. Surgery was needed. The surgeon warned us that kidney tissue are very difficult to work with, and with all the tumors in that kidney, chances were that it would get too messy, and he would have to remove the entire kidney. Laurie and we agreed that we could not leave a cancerous tumor in there. We went ahead with the surgery. Laurie did lose that kidney. Now, everything that is removed in surgery goes to pathology for screening. We never got the pathology report. Several months later during Laurie's annual physical, her primary care doctor mentioned how wonderful it was that pathology found no cancer in the kidney they removed. However, there was a very large tumor that could have caused some serious problems in the near future. Could it be Ste. Anne's Grandson doing His thing again? Oh yes! Now here's the rest of that story!

Because of the removal of her left kidney, Laurie's renal functions are handled by two thirds of one kidney, what remains of the right one, which, by the way, is also full of tumors. Her nephrologists had Laurie seen by a transplant team when her renal function (GFR) dropped to 23. When the function drops to 20 or the creatinine level reaches 2.5, dialysis is required. Once on dialysis, then one's name goes on the list for a transplant. I have to be very honest with you. I do not remember much of what was said during that day that we met with the transplant team. They were very nice people, very intelligent, very competent, and willing to answer any and all questions we had. But I was a wreck. My gut was somewhere between my ankles and my knees. We were setting in motion a life changing process for our Laurie, our baby, albeit a forty-something baby. A kidney transplant today is fairly routine, but is life changing, in that it requires a lifetime of powerful medications, diet, and care. This is difficult for a normal person to handle. In Laurie's case, we are talking about a person with cognitive issues. All this was going through my mind as we met with team member after team member. I don't know how many times I said, "God help us."

He answered.

Incredibly, I should say miraculously, Laurie's levels went up and are still high enough to keep her off dialysis and off the transplant list. Her doctors are at a loss as to how that can be possible since they have trouble finding healthy tissue when they look at her ultrasounds. They may be at a loss, but Laurie, Anna May, and I are not.

Before I move on to share with you the story of Laurie's TSC involvement in her lungs, let me share with you how God has guided us in getting Laurie the best possible medical care available in America. It all began when Anna May discovered the Tuberous Sclerosis Clinic at Mass General Hospital in Boston. The director of the clinic was a neurologist, and as I mentioned earlier, that doctor sent us immediately to a urologist. TSC is a genetic disorder that affects the entire body. It's quite complicated, but in a nutshell, there are two genes that produce an enzyme called M-Tor. This enzyme inhibits the growth of tumors in all the organs of the body. So if one or both of the genes (#9 and #16) are defective and do not produce enough M-Tor, tumors will grow on and in a person's organs. A different type of tumor or defect affects each organ. Some occur in utero, some at a young age, some after puberty. Some of the tumors appear and never grow, while others have a blood supply of their own and grow constantly. Some can be removed, while others, even if removed, grow back. Depending on the severity of the defect of the gene, a person can have such a mild case of TSC as to go undetected, or such a severe case that one can never function and dies at a very young age. Also, it is hereditary. In the last thirty to forty years, since Laurie was diagnosed, research has made great strides in understanding this genetic complex. This research has been made possible through the relentless efforts of brilliant doctors and generous benefactors that have founded clinics such as the Carol and James Herscot TSC Clinic for Adults and Children with Tuberous Sclerosis at Mass General Hospital under the directorship of Dr. Elizabeth Theile, world renown neurologist, in the field of TSC and Epilepsy. This information is important for you to know as I continue to share Laurie's story, a story that involves deep faith as well as great medical care.

Let us return to Laurie's story. At the time her medical care switched from the Lahey Clinic to Mass General Hospital, Laurie was in her late twenties. Soon after the renal surgery, Laurie began to have trouble with her menstrual cycle, and it was discovered that the problem was due to persistent cysts on her ovaries. The ovaries had to be removed, so a gynecologist was added to the team of doctors. Then a heart murmur was discovered, and a cardiologist came on board. That was scary at first, but we were assured that research had found that the TSC involvement of the heart was not progressive, and her heart murmur was not severe enough to cause concern. However, the cardiologist stayed on board for quite a few years. The greatest concern was her kidneys, but soon another area became problematic. Her lungs. When Laurie came under the care of Dr. Elizabeth Theile, a chest X-ray was performed, and small nodules were discovered throughout her lungs. There was good news and bad news. The bad news was that these nodules would definitely affect her breathing capacity. The good news was, research had shown that in women whose lungs are affected by TSC, the nodules, known as "LAM," stop growing and the pulmonary function stabilizes. However, because the research is relatively young, twenty to thirty years, no one can say yet if the lung function could deteriorate at a later age. So, a pulmonologist was added to the team to keep an eye on the lung function. Other members of Laurie's team include an eye specialist, an oncologist who treats her thyroid, a psychologist, and psychiatrist. At a young age, Laurie had dermabrasion performed on her facial nodules, but within a few years, they returned. In her teens, laser surgery was used to remove those nodules that had grown back. They grew back again, and again laser surgery was performed, this time more aggressively. Laurie and we agree, never again. The process was quite painful and because of her age, the nodules, most likely, will not return.

Many of you may be wondering at this point, *how in the world can these people afford this superlative medical care?* Again, God has been exceptionally good to us. Laurie's medical care never cost us one penny out-of-pocket! In the beginning, my employers made excellent health insurance available, then Anna May's employer continued to provide excellent insurance options when my employer did not. Just prior to her becoming an adult, we petitioned the court for guardianship and received it. A few years later, Laurie was accorded disability status. By then, her medical team at Mass General was in place, and they accepted her government insurance.

At this point, I believe that it is very important that Anna May share with you why we know that God is taking care of Laurie, and us, and why our faith remains so strong.

> *In 2011, I attended a retreat entitled "God Changes Everything." It was a wonderful spiritual experience! Prior to the final liturgy of the weekend, I was in the chapel meditating; God's Presence was very real to me. My mind drifted towards thoughts of Laurie and her medical situation when suddenly I felt a VERY POWERFUL voice deep within me say, "I AM TAKING CARE OF HER!" Tears ran down my cheeks as I felt the power of God the Father reassuring me that He is in charge! I came away from that retreat with a renewed spirit and a profound trust that God would continue to provide for all of Laurie's needs.*

Hearing from God, Himself, certainly adds to our hope and peace of mind. Beside Laurie's health, a big worry for us is our advancing age. At the present time, we own our own home, which is quite large, and Laurie has a couple of rooms to herself. The truth is, the house is much too large for people who should be in senior housing. But because Laurie is with us, most places won't take us. The fact that we won't be around forever is a reality that faces us every day. Do we worry what will happen to our daughter after we are gone? Of course we do. But God told Anna May He would take care of her, and I have to believe He will.

Every day I pray for people who do not believe in God. I cannot begin to imagine how they can get through one single day without God in their lives. I cannot imagine my God saying to me, *"No sign will be given to you."* (Mark 8:13) Even when I'm drifting away from Him, when I selfishly turn away from Him and listen to the ancient whispers in the Garden listening to the wrong spirit, God continues to make His grace available to me, providing *signs* that will show me the way back. I've become so dependent on them. They reassure me that He is still there, where He always is.

CHAPTER 11
DAVID & PETER

Psalm 51: 3-4, 11-14

Have mercy on me, O God, in your goodness;
In the greatness of your compassion wipe out my offense.
Thoroughly wash me from my guilt
And of my sin cleanse me.

Turn away your face from my sins,
And blot out all my guilt

A clean heart create for me, O God,
And a steadfast spirit renew within me.
Cast me not out from your presence,
And your holy spirit take not from me.
Give me back the joy of my salvation,
And a willing spirit sustain in me.

Luke 22:33

Peter replied, "Lord, at your side I am prepared to face imprisonment and death itself."

Luke 22: 56-62

A servant girl saw Peter sitting in the courtyard by the fire. She gazed at him intently, then said, "This man was with Him." He denied it saying, "Woman, I do not know Him." A little later someone else saw him and said, "You also are one of them." But Peter said, "No sir, not I." About an hour after that another spoke more insistently: "This man was certainly with Him, for he is a Galilean." Peter responded, "My friend, I do not know what you are talking about." At that very moment he was saying this, a cock crowed. The Lord turned around and looked at Peter, and Peter remembered the word that the Lord spoke to him. "Before the cock crows today you will deny me three times." He went out and wept bitterly.

If I were to choose a Biblical figure as a model for this book, a figure everyone recognizes, and one whose story is that of being very close to God, then turning away, then coming back into favor, then falling back out God's good graces, then repenting again and returning to the loving embrace of God, I would have to choose two. David, a man after God's own heart from the Hebrew Scriptures and the outspoken, yet beloved Peter from the New Testament.

David was chosen as a ruddy youth from the shepherd's fields to be the second king of the Israelites, and the greatest human king Israel has ever known. David's sinfulness is renown as well as his tearful, sincere repentance such as we find in Psalm 51. King David wrote this particular Psalm after being confronted by the prophet Nathan, who came to him after his sin with Bathsheba. At this point in time, David, the man of whom God said, *"Here is a man after my own heart,"* was about as far from God's heart as one can get. Not only had David committed adultery with Bathsheba and gotten her pregnant, but then, in order to cover up his transgression, ordered her husband, Uriah, a soldier, to be placed in battle in such a way that he would certainly be killed. The order was carried out, and the results were what David wanted. However, David was not rotten to the core, and when the prophet came to him and opened his eyes to the fact that God knew what he had done, David crumbled. He knew how far away he had drifted from the Heart that loved him most and loved him unconditionally. Knowing how deeply he was loved, David was able to respond to the grace of reconciliation that God offered him. He repented, sincerely and with great sorrow, wrote this Psalm, begging for God's mercy.

I think it is safe to say that most of us have been there, not necessarily because of adultery or murder, but we have felt so distant from God that it would take a long-distance phone call to reach Him. Like King David, we require His tender mercy and with sincere and contrite heart beg His forgiveness. It's not easy to come crawling back, especially when we seem so far away, and especially if we think it is God who abandoned us. Pride and fear play an awfully large part in the process, keeping us from turning around, coming face to face with God and asking Him for anything, let alone forgiveness. There is an old country music song by the late Ray Price entitled "Lord Help Me." The title lyrics are;

> *"Lord, on bended knees*
> *I'm begging you please,*
> *Help me."*

When we are at the bottom of the pit, at the end of the string, looking up at the hand of God, we are so bereft of everything, where do we find the courage to ask Him for the greatest favor of all, forgiveness? As incredible as it seems, if we look hard enough, we'll notice that the other end of the string is tied to His finger, so He won't let go. We also notice that the string itself is His grace ready to give us the courage to humble ourselves enough to give the string a tug, getting His attention and showing Him our sincere, humble, contrite heart. He forgives us, tugs on the string Himself, and up we go, back into the safe harbor of His hand. O, if only we could stay there. We can, of course. But one thing about that hand and of God, it never closes firmly around us. We are free to stay, or to choose the slippery path of sin and slide off, down and away.

Then there is our role model from the New Testament, Peter, a salty, no-nonsense, tell-it-like-it-is fisherman, who Jesus picked up along the shores of the Sea of Galilee. Hard as nails, brash, outspoken, rough around the edges, here was a man who could take charge and make things happen, but who could also *weep bitterly*. One minute Jesus is patting him on the back for responding correctly in proclaiming that Jesus was the Christ, the Messiah, and the next minute He is banishing him for scolding Him because He, Jesus, predicted His own death and Resurrection. (Matt.16: 13-23) One minute he is shivering in fear because the boat he's in is about to capsize in a storm, and he sees what he thinks is a ghost coming at him, and the next minute he is walking on water. At the top of Mt. Tabor, he is ready to pitch tents for Jesus, Moses, and Elijah. At the bottom of the mountain he is confused by what Jesus said about His Resurrection. After the Resurrection, he hides in fear in the Upper Room. After Pentecost, he boldly preaches about Jesus and fearlessly accuses the Sanhedrin, the elders, the Pharisees, the Sadducees and all the Jews in general of killing Jesus, their Messiah. One minute he's hiding, afraid he will be killed because of Jesus (and he will); the next minute he's being handed the keys that will open the doors of the Church Jesus commissions him to build—and he lays the foundation and begins to build it. He is so much like us it is scary. Would that we would be more like him, strong physically and emotionally, and in his faith and trust in

Jesus. He was a wonderful leader and depended entirely on the graces bestowed upon him by the Holy Spirit, the Spirit that inflamed his soul on the feast of Pentecost. He could be bold, and he could be gentle and understanding. He could be adamant and stick to the rules, and he could be wise and allow new thinking, as he did with Paul and the Gentiles coming into the Church. He depended on prayer to keep himself close to Jesus and what he had been taught by Him. I'm sure he had his weak moments, but in the end, he embraced his fate and embraced the cross humbly and insisted he be crucified upside down because he did not feel worthy of dying as Jesus did. Peter answered the call of Jesus and followed that call to his death.

His call is not so very different than ours. We are called, as he was, to live the Good News and spread the Good News by using the gifts and talents given to us and by relying on His grace to get the job done. Peter, the fisherman, became a bold and powerful preacher, a fisher of men, after receiving the Holy Spirit at Pentecost, taking the message of Jesus throughout the Middle East and into Europe, courageously settling in Rome going head to head and face to face with the conquerors of his homeland and the persecutors of the new Christians. Most of us are not being called to put ourselves in such danger, but we are called, at times to defend our beliefs, as well as to spread the Good News every day of our lives. We are not called to be great orators, fearless preachers and speakers. But we are called to live our lives according to the teachings of Jesus, His Word, His Way, the Way of the Gospel. As St. Francis once said, "Preach the Gospel, and only when necessary use words."

So, how does this call come? Do we get a phone call from Jesus, or an e-mail or text message? We know how Peter was called. Jesus took him right off the boat. But how do we get the message? One of my favorite expressions is, "*We have to be aware and awake to the whisperings of the Holy Spirit.*" These whisperings come in various shapes and forms.

Sometimes they are easy to hear or recognize, but there are times, not so much. That is why it is so important to stay as close to Jesus as possible. We need to be aware when we begin to drift away so we can turn ourselves around and return to Him. Then, it becomes easier to recognize and hear His call. It may come in a sermon, or an unexpected phone call from someone in need of our time or our wisdom. It could be a situation we encounter in our neighborhood or see on television. It could be disguised in a conversation with a friend or acquaintance.

I mentioned an unexpected phone call. I received one just as Anna May and I had decided to slow down, back away from all the commitments that were taking up so much of our time. We were involved in Marriage Encounter, I was involved in preparing High School Juniors for the Sacrament of Confirmation, we were both involved in our parish as Readers of the Word and Ministers of the Eucharist, and we were leading a Bible study group in our home every week. And we were both working full-time jobs. There wasn't much time for Anna May and me. We decided to back off of some of these commitments and began saying "No" to new ones. We no sooner made that decision than the Director of Religious Education in our parish called me. She told me our pastor had asked her to call. He wanted me to head up a new process the Church had instituted called RCIA. I had no idea what that was, so I asked. She wasn't sure either, but knew that it was a process through which non-Christian adults came into the Church. It was basically for converts. I told her that we were not taking on any new commitments, that we were stepping back from stuff, so we could devote more time to our marriage and our five children. When Anna May heard that part of the conversation she asked me what it was all about, so I told her.

All she said was, *"How can you say 'No' to bringing people into the Church?"*

My first chance to say "No," and I couldn't. I said, "Yes."

Since neither of us knew what the process involved, we spent close to two years praying about it and learning about it. The more I learned, the more I was certain that I was not qualified to do this. So I prayed. We all prayed. I had gathered a few friends and formed a committee to simply meet and pray every week for the wisdom and grace we would need to get this started in our parish. After two years, it finally got off the ground, gathered wings, and flew on the breath of the Spirit. It was an involvement that spread over twenty years. Because the catechesis was Scripture based, it helped me expand my knowledge of the Word of God and helped to keep me close to Him. You see, as a teacher, it was more important for the adults in my class to see how I conducted myself on a daily basis, and not just on Sunday. It was very rewarding and quite inspiring. It was beautiful to see the Holy Spirit at work within both the candidates and the catechists. It was a process that inspired growth in all of us involved, and it was a period of time that was easy for me to stay close to God. I was glad I hadn't said "No."

Well, I had said "No," but Anna May reversed that. Thank God.

Chapter 12
Marriage: Walking Together

Hosea 14:2

"Return to me…"

Joel 2:13

Return to the Lord, your God for He is gracious and merciful."

Psalm 30: 12-13

"You changed my mourning into dancing;
Oh Lord, my God, forever will I give you thanks."

Luke 24: 13-35

The two disciples on the road to Emmaus

"How did I ever get to this point, Lord? When did I decide that I had to shed my arrogance, and tone down my ego and start thinking more about You and my family?"

As I thought about the overall swing in my life of being close to God, then drifting away, then coming back, I had to answer those two questions.

As a boy growing up in a small town, in a nice house, in a good, safe neighborhood and part of a good, God fearing family, one might say I was very fortunate. And that would be the truth. I was born into a very loving and faith filled family. At a very young age, my parents introduced me to God, taught me my prayers, and took me to church every Sunday. When I was old enough, they sent me to Parochial school. Eight years later I entered a Seminary at high school level because I felt I was being called to the priesthood. During those first eighteen years of my life, my parents and my teachers did a marvelous job of forming a conscientious spirituality within me. I had grown very close to God and had developed a desire to serve Him as a man of the *cloth*. That didn't work out, and I reentered the secular world. The pendulum began to swing in the opposite direction. I never abandoned my faith or the responsibilities of the religious education I had received as a young boy. I still practiced my faith, but got caught up in trying to decide what I wanted to do with the rest of my life. God became less and less a factor in my decisions. Why? I don't really know. At a time when I should have turned to Him for guidance, I suppose I didn't feel He was all that familiar with what I was capable of doing in the secular world.

Well, I did find something, and I also found someone with whom I could spend the rest of my life, and I am certain He had a role in that even though I didn't seek it. So, despite the fact I was just starting a new career of sorts, and one that didn't pay a great deal, we decided to get married. Very soon children began to fill the house. We had five in the first six years of our marriage. That's an awful lot of responsibility for two young people with very little income. I would take on second jobs that were part-time, or Anna May found work at hours when I would be home. Time for God became very scarce, and I drifted further and further away. Thank God for His grace and for a wife who has always been in tune with the Holy Spirit. She was able to see that I was not only drifting away from

God, but from her as well. I really wasn't contributing all that much to the marriage. She had all the responsibilities, the budget, the kids, and her mother, who lived with us. The balance was way out of whack!

One day she came to me and said, *"Things have to change. I've heard about Marriage Encounter, and there happens to be one soon at the Retreat House in West Springfield. Do you want me to sign us up?"*

I don't know why it sounded good to me. I knew nothing about Marriage Encounter, besides I didn't realize there was anything wrong with our marriage, but I didn't hesitate to say "Yes." We went to that weekend, and I have to say, it saved our marriage. It opened my eyes to the disparity of the physical, worldly responsibilities in our union, and more importantly, it made me realize how far I had drifted from God. Not only was I out of touch with my family, but out of touch with God as well. I wasn't reading Holy Scripture. My only exposure to the Word was at Sunday Mass. And prayer? I was way too busy for prayer. Busy with what? Anna May was doing all the work. I had to change, big time. One of the essential points of Marriage Encounter is to make married people realize that God has to be the center of their marriage. The truth is, because Anna May and I were married by a Catholic priest at a Mass, when we vowed to each other to be married for life, we did so, not only before the best man and the matron of honor and before our families and guests, but also before God. We invited Christ to be a part of our marriage; not only for that day, but also for each day we would be together. I found out marriage is a work in progress. We don't only marry each other on our wedding day, but every day, we are together. Each day, when we awake, we have to decide to love, to love each other enough to be married to each other. Very often this takes the grace of God because, as anyone who has been married for any length time knows, marriage isn't easy. Oh, it looks easy enough, but the reality is very different. It's a lot of work and very often couples need help. We did. The best help we got and still get is from our *"third"* partner, Jesus. I began to realize that marriage was my *"vocation,"* what I was called to do. So, what Marriage Encounter did for us was to teach us how to communicate with each other with respect and loving regard for each other's feelings, and the necessity to rely on and trust in God. In order to trust Him, I had to get to know Him all over again. I soon realized that the best way to get to know Him was through Holy Scripture. That is how He speaks to me and reveals Himself to me. As Anna May and I got more and more involved in Marriage Encounter, the more we saw other ways God manifests Himself to us such as through nature, through other people and their creative gifts like art and music and sculpture and through each individual we meet.

As I gained more respect for what Anna May was doing to keep our marriage alive and our family together, I pitched in more and shared the responsibilities that are part of a Christian family's life. Once we got our relationship healthy again, we became involved in Marriage Encounter on the Team level, and the work involved with that, by its very nature, helped us to keep our spirituality growing, and deepening. It was definitely a turning point in my life.

Following the Marriage Encounter experience, ten years' worth, we backed away and became active in our parish and with The Bureau for Exceptional Children and Adults. Anna May and I also hosted Bible Study groups in our home for many years. The passage from Hosea 14:2, *"Return to me..."* made so much sense. I discovered the beauty in Holy Scripture, and still do. Whenever I decide to turn away from God, or say "No" to Him on any given day, or any given moment, and turn away from Him, like a yo-yo on the way down the string, my conscience has been so fine-tuned by His Word, that I realize what I have done isn't right and that I have hurt the One who loves me more than anyone else. Then, God in His Divine Providence finds a way to have me read a Scripture passage like Joel 2:13, *"Return to the Lord, your God, for He is gracious and merciful."*

Another great Gospel passage that fits in with this theme is found in Luke. It is his account of the two disciples on the Road to Emmaus. (Luke 24: 13-35) I can identify with those guys and I'm sure it resonates with many of you as well.

Let us join that fateful journey of the two disciples who, in their misery and depression, are walking away from Jerusalem and are going back home, downtrodden, because the One who they thought would be the Savior of Israel had been handed over and crucified. They were disappointed and depressed. They had left their home, their jobs, and their friends to follow Jesus, and now He was gone…or so they thought. They thought they had been duped. They thought their hope at salvation was over. Even though they knew that Jesus was no longer in the tomb, they did not believe the reports that He was alive once again. How could that be? So, they decided to walk away. The reports of His being alive again were not enough to peak their curiosity and have them stay just a bit longer. They turned their backs and walked away. But Jesus must have seen something special in them. They must have been good disciples, because He went after them to bring them back. On their way home, Jesus reentered their lives, reminding them of all the prophecies He fulfilled and, in the process, set their hearts on fire.

Isn't this the story of each one of us? We are good people. We are good disciples who believe in Jesus and His Father and the Holy Spirit. Yet we choose to turn our backs and drift away into our material "La-La Land." We are good people, but we get caught up in worldly responsibilities, in worldly pleasures and relationships. We feel the need to be here or there, to see this one and that one, or feel the desire to take a break. Our relationships and our pleasures take precedence, and we walk away from our discipleship despite the fact that we are told that Jesus is alive and well and in need of our presence. We get down and depressed when we lose somebody close to us and we blame God, almost like Martha and Mary, the sisters of Lazarus. But there are times when He knows we are perfectly capable of fending for ourselves, and He really needs us to be somewhere else, doing something else. The problem is, we may not like what He's asking, or we may be afraid of failing and feel unqualified to do what He is asking. Jesus does not call the qualified. He calls the believers, who trust in His grace to handle what He is asking of us. So, as we walk away, He may catch up to us, set our hearts on fire, turn us around and send us back to work. Don't be afraid. You can't out run Him anyway. We know that. Of course, we know that, but we try anyway. That's our sinful nature inherited from our first parents, Adam and Eve. Satan shows us the apple, and we reach for it. Then our conscience bothers us, and we cover ourselves with *fig leaves,* weep and repent.

Since that Garden Event, we have been taught to pray. The Prophets taught us prayers, the Psalmists taught us prayers, Jesus taught us prayers and urged us to pray. The Apostles in spreading the Good News followed suit, entreating us to pray constantly. Because life is what it is, bad stuff happens to us all the time and very often, it is not our fault, and in fact may be no one's fault. It is just bad stuff that impacts our lives and brings us to our knees. Very often, that is when we realize how far we have drifted away from God. It may be not that far, or very, very far, but never ever too far. Remember the two disciples of Emmaus. They had gotten as far as they were going, when something inside them, God's grace, told them to invite the *Stranger* into their home because the hour was late. They soon recognized Him and went running back to carry on their ministry of spreading the Good News. That is each and every one of us in a nutshell. We drift away, He comes after us, sets our hearts on fire, we invite Him in, He heals our hearts and we go running back to Him, and,

"He changes our mourning into dancing;
Oh Lord, our God, forever will we give you thanks."

This has been the pattern in my life. And because I've trusted in Him to take care of my family and me, He has. I am absolutely certain I would never have made it this far if I had not believed and trusted in the love and mercy of my God. I feel closer to God than ever. Sometimes I can feel the clasp of His hand around mine. But because I am weak, I'm like the yo-yo with still a bit of string showing. But He does *change my mourning into dancing,* and although I am a lousy dancer, dancing if far better than bitter tears.

CHAPTER 13
WHAT GOD WANTS

Isaiah 58: 1-11

The house of Jacob cries out to me. They ask me to declare what is due them, pleased to gain access to God. "Why do we fast and you do not see it? Afflict ourselves, and you take no note of it?" Lo, on your fast day you carry out your own pursuits, and drive all your laborers. Yes, your fasts end in quarreling and fighting, striking with wicked claw. Would that today you might fast so as to make your voice heard on high! Is this the manner of fasting I wish, of keeping a day of penance: that a man bow his head like a reed, and lie in sackcloth and ashes? Do you call this a fast, a day acceptable to the Lord? This, rather, is the fasting I wish: releasing those bound unjustly, untying the things of the yolk: setting free the oppressed, breaking every yolk; sharing your bread with the hungry, sheltering the oppressed and the homeless; clothing the naked when you see them, and not turning your back on your own. Then your light shall break forth like the dawn, and your wound shall be quickly healed; your vindication shall go before you, and the glory of the Lord shall be your rear guard. Then you shall call, and the Lord will answer, you shall cry for help, and He will say, "Here I am!" If you remove from your midst oppression, false accusation and malicious speech; if you bestow your bread upon the hungry and satisfy the afflicted; then light shall rise for you in the darkness, and the gloom shall become for you like midday; then the Lord will guide you always and give you plenty even on the parched land. He will renew your strength, and you shall be like a watered garden, like a spring whose water never fails.

This Scripture passage usually appears in a Liturgy at the onset of the Lenten Season. The Church instituted the season of Lent as a forty-day period to remind us how important it is for us to constantly be aware of the snares of the devil whose sole purpose is to draw us away from God. During this time, we are reminded, through Holy Scripture, how aggressive Satan can be in His attempts to separate us from God with the hopes of completely destroying our relationship with Him. During this period of time, it is suggested that we adopt a discipline of sacrifice that will help us to *"turn around"* from our sinful ways; *repent* and turn back to God. Some of us decide to give up candy, or desserts, some to give up their favorite alcoholic beverage; some put aside a dollar or two a day for the poor, and some simply decide to stick to their diets. These are all good things, but are they in the true spirit of Lent? How do praying, fasting, and giving alms draw us nearer to God? The answer is found in Isaiah 58: 1-11. It's not just giving up candy or booze for forty days. It is taking a closer look at our lifestyle and making an honest assessment of how what we do and say expresses our love for God and our neighbor. If we don't like what we see, then it is time to make changes, and resolve to make those changes permanent. Lent is just six weeks long, but the improvements we make in our relationship with God should be permanent, or at least be made with the intention of being permanent. Lent should be a turning back to God and how He wants us to live every day of our lives, not just for six weeks, from Ash Wednesday to Easter. As we turn around and work our way back to God, however way we do that, should become permanent life changes.

Read this passage from Isaiah again. God is talking to him, complaining, actually. He's telling the prophet to go back to His people and let them know He is ticked off with them, because they are nothing more than a bunch of self-centered show-offs. They fast and offer burnt offerings to make themselves look good while they drive their laborers and quarrel and fight with everyone. Then God tells Isaiah exactly the kind of sacrifice He wants. As we read what God wants, it should dawn on us, that these are not sacrifices, these actions should be a part of our everyday thinking and attitudes toward our family and our neighbors…and towards Him! These are traits we need to incorporate into the fiber of our lives. We need to stop looking out for ourselves and begin feeling love and compassion for the guy next door. God gives His list to Isaiah to bring to us;

> *Acting justly; freeing the oppressed; sharing your bread with the hungry; sheltering the homeless; clothing the naked (give a coat to someone wearing only a sweater in zero degree weather, (I have a story about that) and don't turn your back on your own.* (Isaiah 58: 6-7)

God knows what He wants, so, I think it might be a good idea to give it to Him. Here's another good idea. Note this Scripture passage on your calendar every two months, just to refresh your memory.

Here's the story I mentioned above. The last job I had before retiring required me to go into work very early. I would leave the house around 4:00 AM to get to work for 4:30 AM. It was my custom to stop at a convenience store on my way to work and pick up a cup of coffee and a muffin or donut. This one very cold morning, at the beginning of winter, as I went into the store, I noticed a man standing outside, leaning against the building, and drinking coffee. I didn't pay too much attention to him.

As I came out, the man spoke to me. He said, "Hi, cold morning, isn't it?"

I kept walking toward my car as I replied, "It sure is."

As I got into my car I noticed the man was standing with the aid of a crutch. His right leg was missing. Even more striking was what he was wearing, or wasn't wearing. All he had on over his T-shirt was a thin, torn sweater. The left side of the sweater was practically nonexistent. I got into my car, started it up, and was on my way to work. About two blocks away, it hit me like a two-by-four between the eyes. I had two or three winter coats. He, obviously, had none. Unfortunately, time was of the essence, and I couldn't turn back to give him my coat and still be at work on time. I could have given him my coat before leaving the store parking lot. I should have; but was not in tune enough with the Holy Spirit and thought of it too late.

Two weeks later, on a Friday night, I went out to get fish and chips for dinner. I came back to my car with my order, got in and closed the door, when a homeless guy, a known alcoholic, knocked on the window and asked if I had a few dollars extra.

I lied. I said, "No," and went on my way. Why? I could have given him either a couple of dollars, or some of the food I had just bought and gone in for more. Again, I was halfway home when I realized another great opportunity slipped through my fingers. The further away I am from God, the longer it takes for His message to reach me. It is on these occasions, I realize, I need to get closer to Him, so I can hear His message and act on it promptly. Was the lesson learned? Yes. I am now much more aware of the homeless, jobless individuals begging on the busy street corners. We live near a very busy intersection, and often there is a homeless/jobless person with his/her sign looking for a handout. One day, I got curious as to how that person must feel having to beg for the money he needed for rent and food. So, I made a sandwich and added some cookies and a can of soda, put the lunch in a bag, and walked down to the corner. I handed the guy the bag and told him to give me his sign while he took a lunch break. Between bites, he told me what I could do and what I couldn't do. Mostly, I could only stand there and wait for someone to offer me a donation. I couldn't speak unless spoken to. It was very humbling, and I quickly realized that it isn't very likely that anyone would choose to do that unless circumstances forced him or her to.

I'm not sure if you noticed. What God is telling Isaiah to tell His people comes back centuries later when Jesus echoes those same precepts when outlining the questions, we will all be asked at the Final Judgment. (Matthew 25:31-26). So, incorporating these precepts into our lives, not only draw us nearer to God, but also help us to increase in holiness making it more possible that we will be aligned on the *right* with the sheep, thus be invited to spend eternity in His presence.

Chapter 14
Obey, Trust, Love

John 14: 15-21

Jesus said to His disciples, "If you love me, you will keep my commandments. (John 14:15)

"He who obeys the commandments he has from me is the one who loves me." (John 14:21)

This passage begins and ends with Jesus telling us we should love Him and how that love can come about...by keeping His commandments. (John 14:15 & 14:21) But loving someone, truly loving them, is more than just keeping a set of rules they have drawn up for us. Yes, it is true, one way to show our love for Jesus and the Father is to keep the Commandments, but true love goes much deeper than that. There are two criteria I can think of off the top of my head. One is that our love for Him must come from our own free will because of His goodness toward us and not because He has the power to punish us. The second is to love Him unconditionally as He loves us, with no strings attached. That is easy to say, but how can we bring ourselves to love someone we cannot see, feel, or touch? We can love our spouse, our children, mother, father, brothers, and sisters, etc. But God is spirit, unseen, sometimes even very difficult to believe in His existence. So how do we find it within ourselves to love Him? How do we get close to someone we can't see or hear? We know deep within ourselves, there is this unexplainable force that desires to be near Him. We love it when we are close to Him because of the joy in our lives. Everything seems to come up roses. And when we are apart from Him, when we have drifted away, there is sadness, anxiety, turmoil, worry, anger, unrest and all sorts of negative attitudes. We certainly can't see or feel the love that Jesus has for us, never mind feeling love for Him.

As I've pointed out throughout this book, we don't like those negative feelings, and besides, there is that desire deep within us that longs to be near the One who created us. We know the joy of being close to Him. We have felt it, experienced it, and, in His words, *it was good.* We long to be there again; we dearly want to get back on the road that leads to the Father, rocking on the front porch waiting for us to come back. Once we are there again, we don't ever want to go away. We love it there, close to His open Heart. We love Him, the Father, the Son and the Holy Spirit. It is at those times that we wonder why can't we love Him enough to never sin again, to never ever hurt Him again by selfishly turning away from Him. If only we could continue to love God this much for the rest of our lives. We know the peace and the joy of His love for us and of loving Him with such fervor it seems *our hearts are on fire.* How do we remain and abide in that love? How do we maintain a pure heart and soul that wants to keep His commandments and His teachings? How do we stay on the Way to show Him how much we love Him?

For the answer I am going to defer to Pope Benedict XVI who wrote a reflection on this very Gospel passage and he says it far better than I ever could. No matter what religious denomination you follow, these words are for everyone. He wrote:

But what does it mean to love Christ? It means trusting Him even in times of trial, following Him faithfully even on the Via Crucis (Way of the Cross), in the hope that soon the morning of the Resurrection will come. Entrusting ourselves to Christ, we lose nothing, we gain everything. In His hands our life acquires its true meaning. Love for Christ expresses itself in the will to harmonize our own life with the thoughts and sentiments of His heart. This is achieved through interior union based on the grace of the sacraments, strengthened by continuous prayer, praise, thanksgiving, and penance. We have to listen attentively to the inspirations that He evokes through His Word, through the people we meet, through the situations of daily life. To love Him is to remain in dialogue with Him, in order to know His will and to put it into effect promptly.

Pope Emeritus Benedict XVI

There is more, but that is the essence of his reflection of loving Jesus in the deepest possible way, and it involves our entire being and our life in the midst of other people and circumstances, some good, some bad, some indifferent; but somehow, in all of this, we must find Christ, in the people and the events of our lives and give Him thanks and praise for all of it.

Up to this point I have shared with you some major events in my life when I have either fallen away from Christ or come running back to Him, or stayed close to Him, hanging on for dear life. Those types of events are not unique to me, but occur in everyone's life experience, and usually it is not difficult to recognize whether we are distancing ourselves from

God or making an honest effort to return to Him and get as close to Him as we possibly can. What I find difficult is recognizing Him in the day-to-day, nitty-gritty stuff. Something can happen, and I'm totally blind to His presence in that situation. It could be something as simple as the milk for my coffee being sour. Or, it can be as beautiful as a "good morning" hug from my daughter; it might be a compliment from my wife, or my neighbor's cat using my lawn as its litter box; it might be a car who cuts me off at an intersection, or a cheerful hello from a friend; it could be getting the wrong coffee from the drive-thru and not being sensitive to what the server might be experiencing, or the helpful clerk at the hardware store walking me through a maze of parts. This is everyday stuff, and Christ is in every bit of it, everyone and every moment, good or bad, pleasant or irritating. Do I handle them as such? Sometimes. It depends on what mood I'm in.

But here's the thing. My moods, our moods, should not dictate how we handle what happens during the day, and how we act with the people we meet and deal with. I have to remember, Jesus said, *"Love your enemies."* My enemy doesn't necessarily have to be a person. It could very well be a task I dislike very much. I should not allow it to put me in a foul mood. Instead, this would be the perfect opportunity to practice what Pope Benedict said, *"be in interior union with Christ and harmonize my life with thoughts and sentiments through grace achieved by constant prayer and praise; listening attentively to His inspirations."* Whether the job or person is onerous or pleasant, I must remember to make an attempt to recognize Christ and His will for me in the events of my daily routine. That's what it means to love Christ. That's what it means to be close to Him and not want to move away, not one inch, not one centimeter. It isn't easy. Nothing worthwhile comes easily. It requires *interior union with Him and His grace achieved through the sacraments, continuous prayer, praise, thanksgiving, penance and attentiveness to His Word.* This is how

He reveals Himself to us. This is how we get to know Him better. Knowing Him is to love Him. Loving Him is how we stay close to His loving, open heart that will never be closed to us!

Chapter 15

In the Palm of His Hand

Isaiah 49: 15-16

Can a mother forget her infant, be without tenderness for the child in her womb? Even should she forget, I will never forget you. See, upon the palms of my hands I have written your name.

When the idea for this book first began to materialize, I immediately knew what the last chapter would be. However, as time went on it became the next to last. It is the first chapter that got written. Because this episode in my life covered a year and a half and involved quite a few events and many miracles, this is one chapter in which Anna May has a lot of input, her memory for details being much better than mine. This was a time in my life when I was closest to God having put myself in His protective embrace by choice. I moved. And know that I moved. And as time went on, I worked even harder at getting closer. It was a beautiful year and a half and here is what happened.

It all began in early March of 1982. I was working for a local radio station. One of my duties was to do the play-by-play of the High School sporting events. At that time of the year, the basketball State Championship Playoffs were just beginning and the local high school was one of the finalists, and I did the announcing. Play-by-play announcing is a specialty, and the agreement I had with management was that I would get paid a "talent fee" whenever the broadcast was not during my normal working hours. That first game, we broadcast went beyond my normal working hours, so I put in for my "talent Fee." I didn't get it. Payday was Friday, and that was when I found out I would not be paid for that game. I was furious. That weekend, Anna May and I prayed on how I should handle the situation when I returned to work on Monday. I had choices. I could either say nothing and continue to allow management to use me. Or, I could insist I get paid, even though I knew that would not happen. Or I could increase the amount of my talent fee, and if they disagreed with that, I could refuse to announce any other event that occurred outside my normal working hours. That would be 95 percent of the sporting events we covered. I had not asked for a talent fee increase in the 17 years I worked there. I felt if I did that, I would get fired. We prayed. We had five children, and all were teen-agers. The oldest was nineteen, and the youngest thirteen. I was over forty and overqualified in a very limited field of expertise.

As the weekend progressed, Anna May and I felt that God was telling me that it was time for me to stick to my guns, let management know what my true value was, ask for the increase, and if they refused to pay me the talent fee I was requesting, then they would have to hire someone else to cover the sporting events, a major source of income for this radio station. They did what I expected. They fired me! The first thing I did was pray. I had plenty of time to do that since I had to walk home because Anna May had the car that morning. Was I at peace with our decision? Yes and no. You know how those things go. Your mind says, "Lord. I trust you 100%." But your heart is full of fear. I have to admit, I was a bit scared. All we had in our savings account was about $450. Even in 1982, I knew that wouldn't last very long.

As soon as Anna May got home and I told her the news, we agreed the first thing I should do was to go to the unemployment office and apply for benefits. I went that afternoon and was told because I was terminated, I would have to speak to an adjuster. I was shown to his desk. He listened to my side of the story. He then said he would have to speak to my former employer and get his side of the story. When I asked how long it would take before a decision would be made, he told me a few weeks. Wow! How far could we make 450 "bucks" go? For us? Not very far. For God? Well, let's find out.

After about three weeks, that bankbook was pretty much empty, and we had no idea how we were going to buy food for the following week. The next morning, the mailman delivered an inspirational card of hope, together with a small prayer card with a picture of an upright hand, and inside the hand was the figure of a person. Beneath the picture, was this caption: *Isaiah 49*. Neither Anna May nor I had any idea what that meant. She opened the card to see who sent it, and a teller's check for $300 fell out! The card was unsigned. To this day, we have no idea who sent it. Before I tell you what we did with the money, let me explain about the Bible verse. Being unfamiliar with Holy Scripture at that time, we looked up Isaiah 49 in an effort to figure out the intended message of the sender. Needless to say, verses 15-16 explained it very clearly. *"Can a mother forget her infant, be without tenderness for the child in her womb? Even should she forget, I will never forget you. See, upon the palms of my hands I have written your name."*

Immediately we understood! God doesn't move. He is always there. Always.

Now, I will let Anna May explain to you what we did with the $300.

It seemed only logical to me at that time that we should use the money to replenish our empty cupboards and freezer. So,

> we purchased a bulk portion of meat from a local butcher shop. I placed a good deal of it in the freezer, and prepared a variety of meals with the remainder. As I divided everything, I became overwhelmed and began to cry. Denis came into the kitchen at that point and asked what was wrong.
>
> I simply replied, "At a time in our life when we should have nothing, we have SO MUCH." I explained to him that I had difficulty justifying our abundance while a recently divorced mother of five children whom I knew had so little. It became clear what needed to be done. We shared our blessing with this needy family, and God took care of the rest; we NEVER wanted for anything during the entire time of Denis' unemployment.

That was the first of many miracles we experienced during that year and half. Each one helping us to stay so close to God. There were times we could hear His heartbeat. For example, just a few weeks after we shared the meals made from our windfall, we had opportunity to reach out to another need. Again, I'll let her share that incident with you.

> One of my nieces was getting married. The reception was to be a modest one, funded and prepared by my sister. At the time, she was on workmen's comp due to an injury at work. The day preceding the wedding, I called to ask if she would like my help in preparing things. I was taken aback when she informed me that the workmen's comp check she was counting on to pay for the cold cut platters had not arrived. The only cash available to Denis and me at that time was money set aside for our own mortgage payment. While I was speaking with my sister, I hurriedly scribbled a note to Denis ask-

ing if it would be OK to lend her the money. [I will note here that in all of our married life, Denis has NEVER refused me anything!]

Well, my sister and I agreed that instead of lending her the money, I would order the cold cuts and cheese, and I would fix the platters and bring them to the reception. The cost was $50. Following the wedding Mass, Denis and I went home to get the platters, and lo and behold, there was an envelope that had been dropped through our mail slot. Can you guess what was in it? Yes...exactly $50! The donor: unknown (even to this day)!

Praise God!

By then we began receiving unemployment checks, and I had started working two days a week at one of the local TV stations, where a year and half later, I was hired full-time. But unemployment benefits and two days of minimum wage pay is not quite enough to sustain a family of two adults and five teenagers. Somehow it did. Anna May, who handles the budget and the finances, would sit at the table on Friday to pay the bills and look over what was coming up.

She would say, *"Well, the bills are paid, but I don't know what we are going to do next week."*

The following Friday she would finish with the budget stuff and say, *"Well, the bills are paid, but I don't know what we are going to do next week..."*

The following Friday was the same thing, almost word for word.

Week after week, this went on for a year and half. During the week, she would get a call from someone who knew she had a typewriter and would give her work. One time, I got a call from a friend of a former coworker who had a temporary job for me, a couple of days a week for three weeks. Another miracle! Were there bad times? Of course. I was terminated in March, and in early November of that year, I heard of a great job possibility at a local radio station. When I called them, they told me there would be a copywriter (writing commercial ads) position opening after the Christmas and New Year holidays. Wonderful! That was one part of Broadcasting I enjoyed most, creating and producing commercials for sponsors. Well, the holidays came and went. I called the radio station, and they told me they would be making a decision soon. Two weeks later, I called again. They supposedly were still in the decision-making process. Again, I let two weeks go by, then, I called again. This time, I was told the position did not get funded.

Sorry. I was a bit angry. In fact, I was a lot angry. I was so angry I sat down and said to God, *"That's it. You want to play games? You think teasing me like this is funny? Well, I'm going to sit right down and write a Novena to my mother-in-law, Beatrice, and put her on your case. You'll be sorry I sicced her on You."*

For the first twenty years of our marriage, my mother-in-law lived with us. She was the holiest person I had ever known. When she prayed, He listened! I did write a Novena. And I did pray it. No, I don't have it anymore. It got lost over the years. But, I can honestly tell you that, after the fourth day into the Novena, I was at peace with our situation again. I had moved away, so certain I would get that job. Prayer brought me back. God was always there. As usual, I was the one who had moved.

In September of that year, Anna May got a full-time job at Mt. Holyoke. Again, I'll let her tell you how that happened.

> *Time passed by, and Denis' unemployment benefits would soon be ending. I was working part-time at a job with no benefits. One day, I received a call at work from a relative who informed me of a job opportunity at a local college. Upon*

hanging up, I became annoyed by the call, because I liked the job I had, and after all, it was Denis who needed a job—not me. But, I reasoned that I should investigate the opportunity because perhaps it was God intervening. So, I applied and was told I would hear the following week.

A week passed, and I heard nothing, so I called to inquire and was informed that the job had been filled. I hung up the phone and said to God, "If you want me to work there, then YOU let them call ME, because I am not making any further attempts."

Well, just a couple of weeks later, on the Friday evening of the Labor Day weekend, at <u>7:30 pm</u>, I received a call from the Human Resources Department of the college asking if I would be interested in another position. I agreed to interview with them.

As I hung up the phone, I said to Denis, "I have a job at the college."

He replied, "How do you know?"

I said, "Because I told God to have THEM call ME if HE wanted me working there, and, they just called."

Sure enough, I was hired, and I can't begin to enumerate the blessings that resulted throughout the twenty-nine years prior to my retirement from there.

Shortly after that, my unemployment checks stopped. But I was told they would pay for me to go back to school (Holyoke Community College) to learn another trade. One of the classes offered was computer programming. I selected that one, called the college, and registered. I was to begin in two weeks. A few days before classes were to start, the TV station where I was working part-time, offered me a full-time position. It was over. I was back to work. It didn't take long before I realized how close to God I had been for a year and a half and how happy I was and how joyful my heart was during a period of time when I should have been in deep depression. But I wasn't. We never went without. We never went hungry. Our life style didn't change all that much. God watched over us because we are His Beloved.

Remember that $300 check that came through the mail slot? More followed. During the year and half, we must have received close to $1,000 dollars if not more. Some we knew where it come from, most we didn't.

Anna May just kept saying, *"Our bills are all paid, but I don't know what we are going to do next week."* And next week always took care of itself.

"Look at the birds of the air, they have everything they need to eat, and the lilies of the fields. Not even Solomon was dressed as fine of these. So why worry. Worry will not add one day to your life. (Matthew 6:26-30) He fed us and dressed us and kept us warm and dry for a year and half, snuggled safely in the palm of His hand and in His heart. We had moved in, and for a time, the yo-yo didn't move.

CHAPTER 16

ANOTHER JOURNEY

The Book of Ruth 1: 16-18

Ruth said to her mother-in-law, Naomi, "Do not ask me to abandon or forsake you! For wherever you go I will go, wherever you lodge I will lodge, your people shall be my people, and your God my God. Wherever you die I will die, and there be buried. May the Lord do so and so to me, and more besides, if aught but death separates me from you!" Naomi then ceased to urge her to return to her home.

The story of Ruth is one of my favorite stories from the Hebrew Scriptures. Her story foreshadows the adventure of the Magi who traveled a huge distance and found the Babe in an animal shelter in Bethlehem. Ruth, because of her devotion to her mother-in-law, who wanted to return home, accompanied her and found a devoted husband and the One God. The Journey of the Magi ended up pretty much the same way. No, they did not find spouses, but they did find God. The two were led by outside forces. The Magi by a star, Ruth by her love for Naomi, and both found the journey rewarding and worthwhile because of the prize they discovered. I've already offered my thoughts on the Kings' journey. This chapter will focus on the decision of Ruth, a Moabite, to accompany her mother-in-law, Naomi, a Jewess from Bethlehem.

The story of Ruth is a very short book in the Hebrew Scriptures, only five chapters, found between the Book of Judges and the first Book of Samuel. Naomi and her husband, Elimelech and their two sons, Mahlon and Chilion left Bethlehem because of a famine in that land. They settled on the plateau of Moab. The two sons married Moabite women, one named Orpah and the other, Ruth. Soon, Elimelech died, and ten years later, his sons died. Naomi decided to head back to Bethlehem where she had family and friends and urged Orpah and Ruth to return to their families. She was able to convince Orpah, but Ruth made the declaration of love and loyalty that heads up this chapter, *"Wherever you go..."* etc. So, Naomi and Ruth lace up their walking shoes and begin the long trek back to Bethlehem. Once there, Naomi introduces Ruth to Boaz, a friend of the family and the rest is History. Boaz takes Ruth as his wife and they have a son, Obed. Obed becomes the father of Jesse, who in turn becomes the father of David. The great king David. But the greatest discovery for Ruth was her introduction to Judaism and the One true God, the God of Abraham, Isaac, and Jacob. We know nothing at all about the time on the road between Moab and Bethlehem. I was not certain of how long a trip it was so I researched it up on the Internet. All it says is, *about thirty to sixty miles, depending on the route taken. As the terrain is rugged and steep, the trip is estimated to take seven to ten days on foot.* I'm assuming the women joined a caravan headed that way so as not to be traveling alone. They did reach Bethlehem safely, and both women enjoyed a peaceful and fulfilling life.

So why do I include this story as part of this book? First of all, as I mentioned earlier, it is one of my favorite Scripture stories. Of course, it is about a journey, a journey that brought Ruth to a new home, new relationships, and for her, a new God who embraces her, accepts her, loves her, and rewards her with a royal progeny. Earlier I mentioned that Ruth's journey reminded me of the journey taken by the Magi. It was similar in that they both ended up in Bethlehem. There are differences of course. The Magi had no idea they were going to find God, but in coming into His presence, accepted Him immediately, showering Him with very special gifts fit for a king. In the case of Ruth, even before she took one step toward Bethlehem, she had embraced the God of Naomi and vowed to be faithful to Him and Naomi until death. Because of her faithfulness, her intrinsic goodness and devotion, God showered her with gifts. Once she was settled into a home with Naomi, she was blessed with a good job and eventually a good and faithful husband who gave her a son, Obed. She would eventually become the great grandmother of King David. Scripture doesn't tell us if she ever got to know David, but David did exhibit many of the loving characteristics of his great grandmother.

But enough with the history lesson.

Where is the spiritual lesson in this story and how does it fit into this work? It fits because her coming to know God began with a journey. The lesson is found in Ruth's heart, and in the Gospels. Jesus said, *"Whoever loses is life for my sake, will live and whoever chooses life will surely die."*

When Ruth found out that her mother-in-law decided to return to her home in Bethlehem, she made a decision; she chose to put aside all that she had, there in Moab, her home, her family and whatever god she worshipped, to accompany Naomi on the journey and to stay with her and care for her until even she, herself, died and *be buried there with her.* She died to self. She put all of her wants and needs aside and gave herself totally to her aging mother-in-law, to the point of uprooting her own life and reestablishing herself in a foreign land. That is unconditional love and devotion. Before taking even one step toward Bethlehem, Ruth established herself firmly in God's heart. That is the journey that I must take. That is the path I need to follow, even if I have been over it time and time again. Whenever I move away from God and find myself far removed, out in the cold somewhere, on the plateau in Moab, when I come to my senses and realize that it was I who moved, I need to do exactly what Ruth did, die to whatever is within me that is pulling me away from God, get rid of it, turn around and find the path that Ruth took. It is the path that leads straight to God's heart. Having been over that road before, I should be aware of the many distractions that Satan has built up, like huge flashy billboards along the way, hoping to haul me off the track and get me going in the wrong way again. I should be able to recognize the detractors; the phony signs that take me off the wrong exit; the people with empty promises that sound so good; the glittery lights that blind my view of the one *"Light,"* which is my goal, God Himself, *the Light of the World*. This is when I need to rely on His grace to stay in His presence, and keep myself aware and awake to the whisperings of the Holy Spirit and the grace that fills me with the courage and the strength to fight off the temptations of the devil that get stronger and stronger the closer and closer I get to the heart of Jesus.

    The destination is always the same. The location may be different, but the destination is always the heart of God. The Magi found it in the manger in Bethlehem. Ruth found it in Moab when she chose to follow and care for Naomi, her mother-in-law. I have to constantly look within myself to see where I am in my relationship with God. Most often, I know when my relationship with Him is good, when I am really close to Him. There is an inner peace and quiet joy when we are on speaking terms with each other. And then there are times when I am happy, and things are going along quite nicely, but because I believe I am totally responsible for my success and happiness, God and I are miles apart. That is why I need to scrutinize daily, my relationship with God, and recognize my selfish, self-centered attitudes, my need to control my own life. I need to see that, and make a conscious decision to get back on the path that leads back to Him. For me, there are a few ways I can make that happen. There are two Sacraments, Reconciliation and Eucharist; Holy Scripture often jolts me back to reality; Anna May is the one person who keeps my head on straight and my eyes focused in the right direction; and the elderly men and women I minister to every week. God is so present in all of these venues, it is next to impossible to not see Him, to not feel Him, to not desire to be close to Him. I feel as compelled to be near God as Ruth was compelled to be near Naomi and follow her wherever she went. Ruth listened to her heart, filled with God's grace, and knew what she had to do. And there lies the lesson I must learn, to feel the grace of God within me and respond to it. It will never lead me away from Him!

Chapter 17
God, Still You

"You're Still You"

by Linda Thompson & Ennio Morricone
sung by Josh Groban

Through the darkness
I can see your light
And you will always shine
And I can feel your heart in mine
Your face I've memorized
I idolize just you

I look up to
Everything you are
In my eyes you do no wrong
I've loved you for so long
After all is said and done
You're still you
After all
You're still you

This is one of my all-time favorite songs. The reason for that is, although it was not written to be a spiritual song but a love song to a lost love, it is a wonderful reminder of how good God is to me. Not only how good He is, but also how unfailingly good He is. No matter how far away I wander, or attempt to push Him out of my life, He is there when I return to Him. He is there even before I decide to return to Him. He is there because He never leaves. After all, He is still God, faithful and true. He is not just there, floating around in some mystical, ethereal way, unseen and silent. Somehow, when we least expect it, He makes His presence known. When He does, it is usually in a loving manner, most often in gentle unassuming ways. However, now and then, He can be very dramatic, catching our attention and leaving no doubt that He has been on the job and working in our lives. If you have gotten this far into this book, you know I have an example of this to share with you.

This chapter was not planned or intended and was written after I thought I had completed the book. I was waiting for my wife to complete her portion before presenting the manuscript to publishers.

My story begins in November of 2014 with my annual visit to my opthalmologist. As expected, he felt my cataracts were ready to be removed. There was a catch. Back in 1948, I injured my left eye, piercing the cornea. The surgery created a scar, of course, and the injury reduced my vision from that eye considerably, but it was correctable with eyeglasses. So, from the age of nine, I wore glasses and enjoyed good vision. Now this was being threatened by the cataracts that are the bane of most aging eyes. For a healthy eye, like my right one, the surgery is very simple and very successful. However, for my left eye, the surgery would be more delicate and complicated and with greater risks. My doctor told me that he was capable of doing the surgery, but didn't want to since one of his colleagues at Mass Eye and Ear was far more qualified than he was. Repairing corneas was his specialty and, if I agreed, he would gladly arrange an appointment for me to see him and assess what had to be done. I agreed to see this young doctor, confident that if he was sought after and hired by Mass Eye and Ear he had to be good. And, as it turned out, he was very good.

After an extensive examination that involved digital images of both eyes, he determined that two surgeries would be needed. The first one would be to correct the astigmatism created by the scar tissue in the left eye. My cornea in that eye was in the shape of a football. What he wanted to do was make an incision at the top of the cornea hoping it would flatten it out a bit relieving the astigmatism and giving me a good chance at better vision. The second surgery about six weeks after the first one would be very complicated and carry definite risks of low or no success. The reason was that the iris, which is the colored part of the eye and the part that opens and closes depending the amount of light before it. The middle of the iris is the pupil, the black hole in the center of the eye. In my case the iris was stuck to the cornea in the area of the scar tissue making it impossible to dilate the pupil, making it larger enabling the surgeon to remove the cataract and insert a new lens. In my case, the surgery would begin by *unsticking* the iris from the cornea and making the pupil larger, then proceed to remove the cataract and put in a new lens. This young doctor assured me it could be done, that he could do it. I agreed.

And so, we began with the first step, that of reshaping the cornea. He made the incision, and six weeks later, I was back for a refraction to measure the amount of vision my eyes could be corrected to. Lo and behold, with eyeglasses, regular eyeglasses, they are able to correct my vision to 20/20. The doctor couldn't believe what he was seeing. He couldn't believe what I was seeing! He looked at me and said, "I've never done surgery on anyone with 20/20 vision before," and gave me the option of having the second, risky surgery or waiting. I think you all know what option I chose.

Once again, God inserted Himself into my life in a miraculous way. I thank Him for the grace of recognizing that it was His work that brought the young doctor into my life. God was playing chess with my doctors and me. The young doctor came from San Francisco to join the surgical staff at Mass Eye and Ear. My regular opthalmologist was humble enough to refer me to a doctor hired for that very purpose. To me, anyway, the presence of God in this event is an absolute reality; mere humans could never have orchestrated it. There is no doubt in my mind this was His handiwork. Whenever I put on my new glasses, they not only bring everything into focus, they remind me of the grace and gift of vision He has given me; vision good enough to recognize His presence, His nearness to me, and His desire to save my sight. How can I possibly turn away from Him, how can I even think of turning away from Him? How can I even entertain the thought that He had nothing to do with this event, that, after all, it was the young doctor who performed the surgery? Yes, the surgeon made the cut, but his hand was guided by a power far greater than his.

I never, in a million years, thought that a simple action of putting on and taking off eye glasses would make me realize how closely, how lovingly, God cares for me. Yes, Lord, *"You're Still You"*.

CHAPTER 18

ANOTHER MOTHER-IN-LAW

―――――― 1Kings 17: 7-16 ――――――

Then the word of the Lord came to him, saying, "Go now to Zarephath, which belongs to Sidon, and live there; for I have commanded a widow there to feed you." So he set out and went to Zarephath. When he came to the gate of the town, a widow was there gathering sticks; he called to her and said, "Bring me a little water in a vessel, so that I may drink." As she was going to bring it, he called to her and said, "Bring me a morsel of bread in your hand." But she said, "As the Lord God lives, I have nothing baked, only a handful of flour in a jar, and a little oil in a jug; I am now gathering a couple of sticks, so that I may go home and prepare it for myself and my son, that we may eat it, and die." Elijah said to her, "Do not be afraid; go and do as you have said but first make me a little cake of it and bring it to me, and afterwards make something for yourself and your son. For thus says the Lord God of Israel: The jar of flour will not be emptied and the jug of oil will not fail until the day that the Lord sends rain on the earth. She went and did as Elijah said, so that she as well as he and her household ate for many days. The jar of flour was not emptied; neither did the jug of oil fail, according to the word of the Lord that He spoke by Elijah.

No matter what Satan, or life itself throws at us, when we are close to God, when we recognize His grace and presence within us, we can and will make it through. There is a beautiful story in 1Kings that came up in the daily Scriptures a little while back that ignited wonderful memories of my mother-in-law. I reflected on it then, and feel now that it would be fitting for this book.

My wife's parents were married June 9, 1919. I didn't get to know my father-in-law well because he died shortly after I met Anna May. However, I did get to know my mother-in-law quite well because she lived with us the first twenty years of our marriage, and it is this beautiful lady that is the focus of this reflection. This passage from 1Kings is an ancient story. As I was reading and began reflecting on it, it resonated with me more and more because my mother-in-law bore a strong resemblance to the widow in this passage. This Scripture tells us how the prophet Elijah was told by God to go to Zeraphath where *"a widow there, who I have designated, will provide"* for you. So, Elijah, the great prophet, pulls up stakes and goes to Zeraphath, which was also in the midst of a drought. He meets the widow and asks for a cup of water, and as she walks away to get it for him, he then asks for a bit of bread. That stops her in her tracks, and she explains to the prophet that she has only enough flour and oil for a small cake for her and her son, and once they eat that, they will die. Elijah reassures her that if she does what he asks, God will not allow her *"jar of flour to go empty and her jug of oil to run dry."* Without so much as a moment of doubt, she goes and does exactly what Elijah asked her to do. She was willing to give everything she had left to feed this stranger who appeared at the gate of her village. She believed, and she hoped. And God rewarded her faith and her generosity. The story has a happy ending. The three of them, Elijah, the widow, and her son, ate for an entire year before the rains came.

Now, I've read this passage before, but for some reason, when I read it yesterday, all I could think of was my mother-in-law's philosophy. Before I tell you what that is, it is important for you to know that she was the mother of fourteen children, many of them born just before and during the Great Depression. Her philosophy? She used to say, *"If somebody comes to visit, we can throw another potato into the soup."*

As the years went on, I witnessed how close to God this woman was. She was a person of tremendous faith. She never spoke much about her religious beliefs. She didn't have to. She lived them. She didn't read the Bible. She lived it. When she wasn't helping around the house, she would sit quietly in her chair and pray. She prayed for her family and for those who had nothing because she knew how that felt. She never blamed God for the hardships she suffered during the early years of her marriage. In fact, she always gave Him credit for getting them all through those lean years. She was a woman who radiated God's love and joy and peace. One had but to look at her and see the presence of God within her. It was a part of her physical beauty, and I'm sure that is what my father-in-law saw ninety-five years ago. Her positive, humble, happy outlook on life is the perfect example of the power of God's grace. With what she suffered in her life she could have turned into a very bitter, negative person. Instead, her closeness to God and her response to His grace made her a holy, positive influence radiating joy and happiness in the lives of her children, her nieces and nephews, and every one of her grandchildren, plus the many, many people who came to know her in her eighty-two years here on earth, constantly, joyfully answering God's call to live the Gospel message to the fullest. And her *jar of flour never went empty and her jug of oil never ran dry.*

Our jars of flour and jugs of oil are constantly being filled with God's grace as well. We are here because of His love for us, a love we cannot and will not ever be separated from. If that isn't reason enough to work at staying close to Our Savior, I don't know what is.

May you be aware, every moment of every day, of the love, peace and grace of Jesus Christ within you. Alleluia!

CHAPTER 19

CALLING US BACK

Isaiah 58: 3-14

"Why do we fast, but you do not see? Why humble ourselves, but you do not notice?"

Look, you serve your own interest on your fast-day, and oppress all your workers. Look, you fast only to quarrel and to fight and to strike with a wicked fist. Such fasting as you do today will not make your voice heard on high. Is this the fast that I choose, a day to humble oneself? Is it to bow down the head like a bulrush, and to lie in sackcloth and ashes? Will you call this a fast, a day acceptable to the Lord?

Is not this the fast that I choose; to loose the bonds of injustice, to undo the thongs of the yoke, to let the oppressed go free, and to break every yoke? Is it not to share your bread with the hungry, and bring the homeless poor into your house; when you see the naked, to give them clothes to wear, and not hide yourself from your own kin?

Then your light shall break forth like the dawn, and your healing shall spring up quickly; your vindicator shall go before you, the glory of the Lord shall be your rearguard. Then you shall call, and the Lord will answer; you shall call for help, and He will say, "Here I am."

Psalm 86:11

Teach me your way, O Lord, that I may walk in your truth.

Luke 5: 27-32

Jesus went out and saw a tax collector named Levi, sitting at the tax booth; and He said to him; "Follow me." And he got up, left everything, ad followed Him. Then Levi gave a great banquet for Him in his house; and there was a large crowd of tax collectors and others sitting at the table with them. The Pharisees and their scribes were complaining to His disciples, saying, " Why do you eat and drink with tax collectors and sinners?" Jesus answered, "Those who are well have no need of a physician, but those who are sick; I have come to call not the righteous but sinners to repentance,"

It's party time at Matthew's house! His Jewish name was Levi, and he was not a very loved man. He was IRS. Yes, the taxman. In the eyes of the Jews, he was a grave sinner, whale poop. But Jesus called him! "I want you to follow me." Oh, Jesus was in for a bad time because of this one. But as usual, He handled it beautifully, putting the Pharisees and scribes in their place with the response;

"Those who are healthy do not need a physician, but the sick do. I have not come to call the righteous to repentance but sinners." (Luke 5:32)

Levi, known to us as Matthew, Apostle and Evangelist, was as far removed from God as one can get. But in the blink of eye, in the soft whisper of an invitation, *"Follow me,"* Matthew leaves his job, his sole source of income, to follow Jesus. He is so changed by these two words, *"Follow me,"* that he gathers his friends and relatives and throws a huge party. I know I don't have to tell you about the joy that you feel when you repent, then forgiven, come back to Jesus. Isn't it true, the further away we have wandered, the greater the joy when we return? One thing we have to understand is that Jesus is just as happy, if not more so, to have us back. This is the time, the season for us to make that decision to move closer to Him. No matter how close to God we think we are, there is always some space between us that we can close up. That is why the Church offers us such wonderful Scripture passages as those above. Isaiah is told by God the Father to go and teach His people how important it is for them to come back to Him, and how they should go about it. At this particular time in their history, the Israelites had been released from Babylonian captivity and were trying to rebuild their homes, their lives and their traditions. They were distant and now they were returning and God the Father was using Isaiah, the prophet, to give them the guidelines they would need to help them reestablish themselves in their former homeland. That's us. We can use those same guidelines. When we are at a loss as to what kind of sacrifices God wants from us, read the above passage from Isaiah, chapter 58. God is responding to His people's complaints and lets them know, in no uncertain terms, exactly what He wants. We will, then, be following His way. Yes, we will stray and even get lost at times. We'll be in good company though, such as King David. Pay attention to what he wrote in Psalm 86:11,

"Teach me your way, O Lord, that I may walk in your truth."

That is great advice when we *turn around,* repent and choose to find our way back to Jesus, and *follow Him.* We never have to worry about finding Him either. He is where He's always been, in our hearts. He's not the one who moved. We are the ones who choose to move away. And just so you know and don't go around boasting, it is through His grace that we hear His voice calling us back. Yes, His voice. It could be through a relative, through a friend, a minister, a priest, something on the Internet, and very loudly, through Holy Scripture, The <u>Word</u> of God. Once again, I offer this advice; *be aware and awake to the whisperings of the Holy Spirit!* Praise be to Jesus Christ, King of endless glory!

CHAPTER 20
THE BE-ATTITUDES

Matthew 5: 3-12

The Beatitudes

When I wrote this chapter, I intended it to be the last because I wanted to end this book on a positive note. Maybe it's the joy of being close to God while writing this that inspired me to write two more chapters. Anyhow, there is no question that our faith journey is fraught with many twists and turns, peaks and valleys, as we move away from God and back again. There are many reasons for this to and fro, some valid, most not so valid. And our journey back to God can also be motivated in various ways. As we have seen in previous chapters, repentance and seeking forgiveness is one of the most common ways of getting back on the path that brings us into the presence of God. But that is not the only way. I would like to end this book by making everyone aware of the various positive ways we can work our way closer and closer to the *"open"* heart of Jesus, and become holier in the process. I was *urged* and *encouraged* to take a closer look at the various ways we either stay close to God, or work our way a little bit closer on a regular steady basis. There is no doubt that we are sinful people and require forgiveness every day. But most of us are not bad people. We don't willfully turn away from God, and when we do hurt Him, many times it is not a premeditated act; it is a spur of the moment thing, the result of a rash decision, done without much thought in the midst of a busy, stressful incident. We immediately realize we have come up short, and what we have thought, said, or done certainly did not praise or please God. We quickly ask Him to forgive us and move on. We enjoy being close to Him, and we do our best to stay there, or even better, move a bit closer. How do we do that? There are so many ways. There's prayer of course. Let us explore that for a moment.

Rote prayer is always good, especially the prayer Jesus taught us, the *"Our Father."* However, when we realize that *"prayer"* is communicating with God, we can simply sit quietly and talk to God about anything and everything. He loves to chat. Then there is active prayer, when we do something, anything really, and do it in His name. It can be something as simple and mundane as sweeping the floor, or picking up something someone dropped. When we encounter someone we don't like very much, we can take the time to greet him or her and chat with him or her briefly but kindly instead of being curt or rude, and do it in the name of Jesus. When something or someone angers us, we can develop a habit of pausing for just a brief moment before acting rashly, taking that moment to ask God to temper our reaction and respond with patience and understanding. Here's another great prayer. Offer your entire day at work as a prayer for those who are jobless and homeless. Prayer doesn't necessarily require words. Your actions, the things you do, can be very effective prayer. All it takes is to recognize the moment and say, *"Lord, this is for you."* Whether it is something that takes very little effort on our part or something that is very difficult and involves hard work and sweat, when it is done in His name and for His praise and glory, we take a huge step closer to Him.

Reflection, journaling, meditation, and contemplation are very effective prayers that bring us closer to God. Mostly every day I try to meditate on the Scripture passages chosen for the Liturgy of the day. I find that it helps my spiritual life when I put on paper what I feel the Holy Spirit is saying to me through the Prophets, Psalms, and Gospels. Then, before going to sleep at night, I look back on my day and use the reflection I wrote to see if I've lived up to it. Very often, the reflection takes on an entirely different aspect, and brings me deeper into the richness of the Word.

Journaling requires meditation, a way that Anna May chooses to pray frequently. Once she begins to write, she very often reveals things about her spiritual life that surprise her. Here's a perfect example from her journal dated June 27, 2014.

> *Personal revelation: My EGO is the root of my sin!*
> *It doesn't let me forgive those who have hurt me.*
> *It makes me want to be better than everyone else.*
> *It makes me hold grudges.*
> *It is the root of my negativity.*
> *It is the root of my pride.*
> *WOW!*
> *EGO is the enemy!*
> *"Work on this, Anna May."*
> *"How, God?"*
> *"<u>Practice humility.</u>"*
>
> *Look to God as your focus. Live for God each day. GOD is the answer.*
>   *OK God, I get it. I drifted while I was working. We need to get back in touch. <u>I moved</u>, not You.*

I thank Anna May for allowing me to use her personal journal as a wonderful example of how we can discover, even measure the distance between God and ourselves. This sharing also emphasizes the need to listen for the voice of God who willingly, lovingly enters into conversation with us, suggesting how we can improve our relationship with Him.

Contemplation is very similar. The criteria for contemplation is to put oneself in the "*now.*" That is, to remain in the present moment. Don't think about the past; don't worry about the future. One must find a very quiet place where there are no distractions. It helps to find a comfortable position, close your eyes, and just *be*. Thoughts will come, of course. Allow them to be there, but then let them go and return to your center. Many people choose a "*mantra*", a one- or two-word phrase that helps them to get back to their inner self. It is not an easy form of prayer. It sounds easy, but for many it is very difficult to either stay awake, or to not dwell on the thoughts and problems that present themselves. This is one form of prayer I have a great deal of difficulty with. On the other hand, Anna May loves it, and it is one of her favorite ways to pray. The truth is, it is in the peace and quiet that God comes to us. It is there we find Him and begin to understand what Jesus meant when He said to His Apostles at the Last Supper;

> "*A little while now and the world will see me no more; but you see me as one who has life, and you will have life. On that day you will know that I am in the Father, and you in me, and I in you.*" (John 14:19-20)

You can't get much closer than that!

Obeying His Commandments is another way of staying close to Him. Jesus often tells us that is necessary for getting into the Kingdom of Heaven. And that's where He is. We all know the Commandments and from day to day we do our best to comply with the demands they put on our thoughts, words, and behavior towards God and neighbor. Even though some of the things Jesus asks us to do throughout the Gospels seem to be next to impossible, we do our best from day to day, relying on His grace to help do His will. Some of the things He asks us to do are to *wash feet* as He did; to *serve, rather than be served;* to *feed the hungry;* to give *a drink to the thirsty;* to *clothe the naked;* to *visit the lonely and the imprisoned;* to *love our neighbor, AND our enemies;* to *act justly, love tenderly, and walk humbly with our God.* These are all part of the Ten Commandments, and Jesus is simply showing us how to live them out to their fullest extent. Another one of His teachings we need to really pay attention to in our effort to remain close to Him appears in the Sermon on the Mount, the Beatitudes, Matthew 5: 3-12. As good as the Beatitudes are, Saint Ephrem, a 4th century hermit, understood how we could incorporate them into the fabric of our daily lives. This meditation appeared in *The Magnificat,* a daily devotional published by the Dominicans.

Living the Beatitudes
By St. Ephrem the Syrian

Blessed is he who in the Lord has become free of all the affairs of this vain life.

Blessed is he who has in mind the coming terrible judgment and tries to heal the wounds of his soul with tears.

Blessed is he who in tears has become like unto a cloud, and daily uses them to extinguish the fiery flame of the evil passions.

Blessed is he who excels in good measures of ascetic feats, hoping to receive from God the heavenly Kingdom.

Blessed is he who like a fire is ablaze with love and has burned up in himself all impure thoughts and corruption of the soul.

> *Blessed is he who has found a choice heavenly pearl and, having sold everything that he had on earth, has bought this one jewel.*
>
> *Blessed is he who has found a treasure hidden in a field, rejoiced and cast aside all, and acquired this one piece of land.*
>
> *Blessed is he who ceaselessly remembers the day of his departure and strives to be ready and fearless on that hour.*
>
> *Blessed is he who finds boldness in the hour of his leave-taking, when the soul with fear and trembling bids farewell to the body, for the angels shall come to take his soul, to separate it from the body and place it before the throne at the immortal and terrible judgment place.*

Saint Ephrem the Syrian

The words of Jesus, delivered to a throng of thousands, echo down through the ages and touch our lives today. It is one thing to read them and acknowledge their significance, and quite another to incorporate them into our everyday choices. It is one thing to read a meaningful meditation like that of St. Ephrem, and quite another to spend time meditating ourselves on those same words of Jesus and discover what they mean for us and truly do our best to live them out. That is where the battles are won. We must pay attention to what the Gospels are saying and take the time to discover what they are specifically saying to us as individuals. It is these discoveries that keep us close to God as we welcome His grace to help us survive the nitty-gritty things of everyday life that force us to make decisions. When we rely on His grace, we are bound to make the right choices and stay cozily nestled in the warm, loving embrace of our Savior, close to His *open heart whose door will never close.*

One night as I was about to fall asleep, a question popped into my mind and suggested to me that it would be a good AMEN to this chapter and book. Here's the question:

How do I feel about my relationship with God—Father, Son and Holy Spirit?

Here's my answer.

How do I feel about my relationship with God? I honestly have to give that serious thought, and I don't think I can do justice to that question in one sitting. However, once the question presented itself to me, I knew I had to make an effort to respond. One thing I am very certain of; God loves me way beyond what I deserve, and I certainly have done very little to earn His goodness toward me. Yes, I try to be faithful to Him, but during the course of a single day, I fail way too many times. I know I cannot be pompous about my faith in Him. Yes, I do believe in Him and in His Son and in the Holy Spirit, but I also know that that faith comes from Him, from a well-spring of grace given to me freely and that I am not worthy of it. I am very well aware of the fact that I have done nothing of value on my own; that if I have ever done anything worthwhile it is only through His grace. I can never take credit for it. I cannot even take credit for my relationship with Him. When it is good, it is because of Him. When it is bad, it is entirely my fault. So I do relish the good times, for it is when I am closest to Him that I am the happiest. And I know that is when He is the happiest with me. I love this quote from the book *Jesus Calling* by Sarah Young. She says, *"The Kingdom of God is not about earning and deserving; it is about believing and receiving."*

I am well aware of the fact that He loves me far more than I can possible love Him, and I believe what St. Paul wrote the Romans:

> ***"I am convinced that neither death, nor future things, nor powers, nor height, nor depth, nor any other creature will***

be able to separate us from the love of God in Christ Jesus our Lord." **(Romans 8:38-39)**

Because of His unconditional, unfailing love for me, I trust Him 100 percent. I have come to depend on Him, not only for big stuff, but for day-to-day things as well. I'm talking about little fits of temper, spurts of bad language, ignoring the homeless person at the busy intersection hoping for a few dollars, insensitive comments that hurt those I love, not visiting often enough those who are homebound. In a nutshell, being selfish. I know Jesus can help me with all of this. Not only can He help, but is willing to help at a moment's notice, because He is always present in my life, and I know that. That is so comforting. I can talk to Him anytime I choose, whether or not I'm happy with Him. There are times when I'm very disappointed with Him, and He knows that, yet He doesn't turn away when I confront Him angrily expressing my discontent. He lets me vent and blow off steam. He patiently listens.

When I finally run out of steam, I sit back and listen. On a few occasions, I've heard Him respond, *"Denis, Denis, why are you so upset? Don't you know that this is for your own good?"*

All I can think of is how He addressed His good friend, Martha, when she complained to Him about her sister Mary. Wow! Am I that good a friend of His?

"I take your word for it knowing it is for my own good and somehow I'll make it work for me, just show me the way."

I realize that I must depend totally on His love for me and that I can't possibly ask too much of Him. He wants me to come to Him. The perfect example of that is a bit of a long story, but I'll try to shorten it up for you. Recently a nephew who lives about four hours away from where we live asked my wife to house sit and dog sit and visit his mother, who is in a nursing home, while he was away. Anna May agreed to do it. His mom is Anna May's sister. Our daughter was back to work, and so I could not accompany Anna May on the two-week sojourn. She would have to travel there alone and stay there alone, albeit with a couple of very protective dogs. I prayed. I didn't know for what. I just prayed. Then, suddenly, a recently widowed friend of ours expressed the need to get away for a while. Anna May invited her to join her on the Jersey Shore where our nephew lives. His house is on a beautiful lagoon in a quiet neighborhood. Perfect. God answered my prayer. Then, He seemingly unanswered them.

The friend developed a health problem and would not be able to accompany Anna May. So, I had one of my chats with Jesus. I was disappointed, but not angry. I had a feeling that, somehow, He was going to take care of the situation, that our friend's health procedures would be postponed or changed so that she would be able to go with Anna May. Every time I would pray, I had the feeling that I needn't pray about that situation and to pray for something of greater importance. OK. Still concerned about our friend's need to *"get away,"* Anna May investigated a Maine vacation and sent the details to her. The next morning, as I was leaving for the golf course, the friend called. I gave the phone to Anna May and left. All during that round of golf I had the feeling her medical plans were rescheduled. Guess what? When I got home, I was greeted with a smiling Anna May and the good news. How can I not feel good about my relationship with God when He treats me so kindly, so lovingly?

I do tend to be a bit self-centered, but my relationship with God is not good or bad depending on how He answers my prayers. Of course I feel good when He answers them, as He did in the sharing above. But that is not what defines how I feel about my relationship with Him. Until a few years ago, my relationship with God was basically one of awe and reverence. He was *"the Man upstairs,"* the Almighty who would either welcome me into heaven or condemn me to Hell. I believed in Him, I loved Him and tried my best to serve Him and not hurt Him or let Him down in any way. It was very neat, very safe. He was the Boss and as was my ilk I kept my *"superior"* at arm's length. Then I retired and saw how Anna May prayed every morning and witnessed her wonderful, comfortable relationship with all three persons of the Holy Trinity. I was envious. I set out to improve my relationship with God. I began attending daily Mass and reading the Scripture passages chosen for that Liturgy. Then, through Anna May, I became familiar with Lectio Divina and began reflecting on the Scripture passages I was reading every day. The more I reflected, contemplated, and meditated on the Word, the more familiar I became with the love of the Father, the friendship of the Son, and the wisdom of the Holy Spirit. I actually got to be on speaking terms with all three without losing the reverent respect I had for Them. And then one day my whole world was turned upside down.

During my morning prayer, I read Psalm 139: 1-18. By the time I got to verse 18, I was in tears. I was especially touched by verse 14:

"I give you thanks that I am fearfully, wonderfully made..."

I never really considered myself fearfully, wonderfully made at any time in my life. I do have a healthy ego, and I do struggle with pride. Humility is not my strongest virtue, yet I never saw myself in the same light as God sees me. As much as I love Holy Scripture, I have difficulty remembering chapters and verses that are important to me and very often I have to rely on my Concordance to find what I'm looking for. But not Psalm 139. You see, God began *"forming my inmost being and knit me in my mother's womb..."* (PS. 139:13) in the fall of 1938. God was finished with His knitting in July of 1939 when I was born. How can I forget Psalm 139? That is so intimate, so loving, I will always remember verses 13 and 14. I don't know all of the 18 verses of the Psalm by heart, but I know what they say and what God wants me to know about how much He wanted me and loved me, then and now, and until I return to Him.

I have come to realize that it is my responsibility to return to Him what He knitted as undamaged as possible. In fact, I am working hard at returning His knitting better than it was in July 1939. Like the parable of *"The servants and the Talents,"* I am striving to return with twice as much as I was given. What else happened to me after reading that Psalm, once I stopped crying? I was able to talk to God in my own words, as easily as I talk to Anna May. I can speak to Him as a friend and lover. I've known for some time that I am His *"beloved,"* and now I am very much aware of how deeply that love goes. That forces me to become aware of how much I love Him in return and how hard I have to try to continuously make that love grow. I have found that reflecting and meditating on His Word helps me to find new ways of expressing my love for Him. On the flip side, I am now more sensitive of how much my sinfulness hurts Him. This encourages me to work harder at resisting temptation and curbing my impulsiveness. As a result, my language has improved, my thoughts have improved and my attitudes, hopefully, reflect a more Christian life.

I love my present relationship with God and I work very hard at keeping it that way. Satan doesn't like it though, and that is what forces me to work so hard. There are so many distractions he can use and directs them at my weakest areas. However, lately the Holy Spirit has helped me to realize that when my weaknesses are assaulted, that is Satan's work, and all I need to do is say a quick prayer to Jesus, or just think of Jesus, who will immediately come to my assistance. Why did I not listen to the Holy Spirit earlier in life? Good question! At any rate, I am so thankful to be able to recognize the presence of God within me and to willingly use the strength of His grace to accomplish the simplest of things that reflect His love and keep me close to His Sacred Heart.

Epilogue

From the letter of Paul to the Romans
8: 35-39

Who will separate us from the love of Christ? Will hardship, or distress, or persecution, or famine, or nakedness, or peril, or sword? As it is written, "For your sake we are being killed all day long; we are accounted as sheep to be slaughtered."

No, in all these things we are more than conquerors through Him who loved us. For I am convinced that neither death, nor life, nor angels, nor principalities, nor present things, nor future things, nor powers, nor height, nor depth, nor any other creature will be able to separate us from the love of God in Christ Jesus our Lord.

Who moved? I hope this little book has convinced you that when you feel distant from God, it wasn't God who moved. So, then it had to be you... or me. Never God. Through our own sinfulness, we draw further and further away from Him. And then, when we are so far from Him, we can't feel Him, or hear Him, or see Him, we go so far as to blame Him for abandoning us. We are so foolish, aren't we? We are the ones who moved.

God is solid, like rock. The above passage from the letter of St. Paul to the Romans is one that we need to earmark, copy it, write it down somewhere, save it, reread it, over and over again, especially if we tend to blame God for deserting us and turning His back on us. My dear friends, that is impossible. It will never ever happen. As one gets older, the truth of this becomes more and more evident. Verses 38 and 39 stand right up there among my favorites. They are a convincing argument that I am the one who moves away from God, for He would never, ever move away or remove Himself from me. Not that I deserve to have Him present within me, for never am I that deserving.

But He has promised to be with me always and, as we know, God keeps all His promises. Breaking a promise is sinful, and He is incapable of that. So, regardless of my level of worthiness, He remains with me and in me. And like Paul,

> *"I am convinced that neither death, nor life, nor angels, nor principalities, nor present things, nor future things, nor powers, nor height, nor depth, nor any other creature will be able to separate us from the love of God in Christ Jesus our Lord."*
> (Romans 8:38-39)

That doesn't even begin to cover all the bases, but the same is true for anything else you could possible think of, like sinfulness and war, and politics, and disease, and powerful enemies, etc. etc. Nothing, absolutely nothing can keep God's love away from us. I repeat, when we feel distant from God, and many times throughout our lives we will experience a great distance, remember, GOD IS NOT THE ONE WHO MOVED! Even though we are the ones who move, it is always His grace that makes us aware of the distance between us, and His grace that fills us with the desire to return to Him. He doesn't force us to close the gap. He simply offers His grace, and we can refuse it or accept it. No matter how often we refuse it, it is always there, as gift and blessings for the taking, and He welcomes us back with open arms. Remember, *nothing is able to separate us from the love of God in Christ Jesus our Lord.* Got it? Keep it! Amen and Alleluia!